Albatross & Her Crew

Fifty years of floundering in Cape Cod Bay

By

Scott E. McDowell

The first of 100 Albatross Deck Hands

Paperback edition: ISBN 978-0-99095-654-9
Kindle edition: ISBN 978-0-99095-655-6

Available from Amazon.com, Createspace.com
and other retail outlets.

View Scott's other literary works at:
www.scottemcdowell.com

Email Scott to purchase signed copies:
scott_e_mcdowell@yahoo.com

Cover design by E.K. King

Revision 1 – April 2018

Contents

Sponsors

Albatross & Her Crew

Fifty years of floundering in Cape Cod Bay

Scott E. McDowell

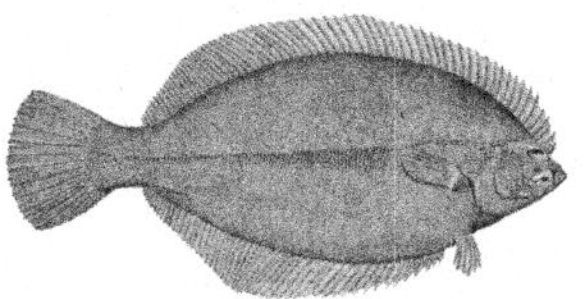

1
Introduction

The *Albatross* is a 'Head Boat' that takes summer tourists bottom fishing in Cape Cod Bay to catch flounder and I was the first Deck Hand, over fifty years ago. The large gray boat is well known in Dennis and neighboring villages because it's been running since 1965. Imagine over 5,500 four-hour fishing trips and 220,000 passengers of all ages stepping off the boat with big smiles, each with a bag of fish in their hand.

It's certainly not 'deep-sea' fishing nor are the trips geared for giant tuna, great white sharks or whale watching. But it's a perfect family excursion for young children to catch their first fish at sea. Parents enjoy the leisurely trip with no worries, as Deck Hands skillfully direct the on-deck activities, handle the fish and untangled the lines.

The boat and its daily schedule are so well known by five generations of Dennis beachgoers that many mothers consider the *Albatross* their timekeeper. Their teen children are to return home when the boat can be seen heading back to Sesuit Harbor late in the afternoon. Some families also view the *Albatross* as the ideal first summer job for their son or daughter. I and three of my cousins worked on the *Albatross* and remarkably, one-hundred Deck Hands have worked summers aboard, since it began operation. The boat has become a legend, as have the various Captains who barked orders to the young Deck Hands.

The *Albatross* is still operating during summer in Cape Cod Bay. Go on a fishing trip – become part of history. Better yet, have your son or daughter become the next Deck Hand. Visit www.albatrossfishing.com

2

Dennis Village in the 1960s - before Regulations

The quaint village of Dennis, first settled in 1639 on the shores of Cape Cod Bay, was idyllic for teen boys in the early 1960s. The village was initially referred to as North Dennis, within the Town of Dennis (incorporated in 1793) that extends like a belt across the Cape, from the Bay to Nantucket Sound. North Dennis is shortened to just Dennis by locals and for hundreds of years, they've had an 'attitude' (some say conceit) that their quaint, non-commercial village is the gem of the town. Additional fuel to their argument is that the Cape Playhouse was established in the village in 1927. Truth be told, East Dennis likely gained more national recognition and fame in the mid-1800s when sleek 'Clipper Ships' were built in Sesuit Creek during America's Golden Age of Sail.

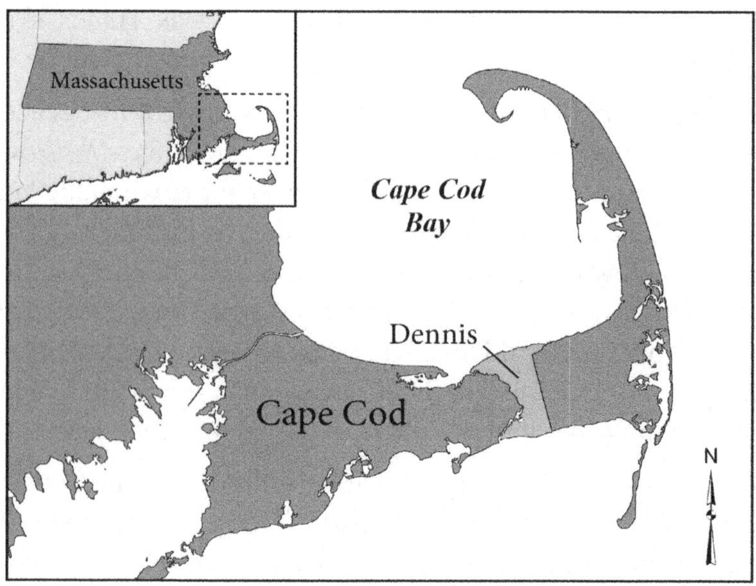

Distances in the small village were short, with most families living within one mile of the town center, defined by the grocery store, Post Office, Dennis Union Church, cemetery and gas station – all the essentials of life. A small number of family names (e.g., Crowell, Howes, Sears, Hall and Thatcher) are etched into the majority of lichen-covered gravestones in the Dennis Village Cemetery, dating back to 1728. Many distinguished citizens of the town can be found there, including Reverend Josiah Dennis (died 1763), for whom the town was named. Also, Asa Shiverick, founder of the local shipyard and his sons, David, Asa Jr. and Paul who produced the only clipper sailing vessels built on Cape Cod.

Hyannis, located about eight miles to the southwest, was considered a city by Dennis folk, and they made the 'long' trip as seldom as possible, mainly to purchase clothes and hardgoods. I remember back to the 1950s when an old but energetic Dennis woman named Clara Belle Sears would walk briskly to Hyannis and back for shopping. She would never accept a ride, even from friendly motorists on rainy days. As kids, we chuckled about her name because Clarabell the Clown was a celebrity on one of our favorite television shows in those days. Clarabell, initially played by Bob Keeshan of Captain Kangaroo fame, was the mute partner of Howdy Doody.

For the teen boys of the village, winter months required attention to schoolwork but they could easily bike to each other's house for indoor activities or to the horse pasture behind 'Old Ernest' Crowell's house for afternoon baseball when the weather was permissible in spring and fall. For boys like myself, all that mattered was summer – at the beach, saltwater fishing and eventually, boating without our parents aboard.

Back in those days, winters were much colder than present day climes. Fifty years ago, Scargo Lake froze over many weeks each winter; sometimes longer during extended snowless periods as cold, Artic air blanketed the Cape. There was an old icehouse (barn) at the northeastern end of the lake, owned by Anson Howes who would cut blocks of ice from the lake in the dead of winter. Inside the icehouse, he covered the ice with sawdust to slow the melting process.

The first refrigerators with freezer compartments arrived in Dennis around 1920. By the late 1950s, most families had small freezers so ice was no longer harvested from the lake.

When new ice-cover had persisted on Scargo for a week or longer, the 'North Side' Volunteer Fire Department would make a quick check of ice thickness for the safety of village skaters. As soon as 'word got out' (before emails or Facebook posts) that the ice was sufficiently thick over much of the lake, parents allowed their teen boys to skate or play hockey.

Most memorable were the homemade iceboats that would streak across the lake at speeds up to forty miles per hour, with no brakes. Evasive action consisted of a full turn with the crude rudder (often a rear ice skate) before the abrupt shoreline was encountered, less than a half-mile across the lake. Also very exciting were the evening skating parties, attended by many of the village residents. For these events, a dozen old car or truck tires (without metal rims) were obtained from the local auto garage and used to fuel a large bonfire. The tires were heaped into a pile near the center of the lake, doused with gallons of gas and the whole pile was set ablaze with a loud 'womppp' that jolted the young skaters backward by the shockwave of ignition. The instant bonfire was a tremendous source of light and much-enjoyed heat within fifteen feet of the blaze, although the smoke and soot were overwhelming for anyone who skated downwind of the inferno. Children quickly learned the difference between upwind and downwind directions. There were no environmental police to establish a wide perimeter around the blaze with yellow WARNING tape.

The tires burned through the night unattended and no one was concerned – it was just normal activity back in those days. Life was simple and fun for the village boys. The concept of environmental police was not even a dream in the minds of the local Authorities.

Furthermore, Dennis life was not cluttered with regulations, nor was there concern about air pollution, climate change, seat belts in cars, bicycle helmets, dog leashes, cigarettes, etc. Town folk just did what they did and parents set their own rules for their children's safety and behavior; risky or not.

When we swam in the lake during summer, the coils of tire reinforcement wire were easily spotted in a pile on the lake bottom. No problem with this either, as the metal lay in deep water, out of swimmer's harm. It was the attitude of the 1960s – no need to worry about the small stuff. Eventually, the rust dissolved and its contribution to the dissolved iron concentration of the large lake was likely undetectable, even with today's mass spectrometry analyses.

The purpose of this reminiscing is to stress the absence of environmental regulations back in those days. Returning focus to Cape Cod Bay, there were no limits on saltwater fish catch either; no recreational fishing license required. No limits on flounder size, how many clams you could dig at low tide, not even limits on how many seaworms you could gather for bait, but they're all tightly specified in today's regulations. Nor was there major concern about the number of striped bass you could legally keep, nor how many barrels of herring you could harvest with long-handled dip nets from Stony Brook Creek at the Brewster Herring Run near Easter time. Local lobstermen would fill up as many barrels as they could carry in their pick-up trucks each night after work from their day jobs. It was free lobster bait without interference from environmental police or game wardens.

There weren't even limits on how many giant bluefin tuna you could land, presuming you were skilled enough to catch these monsters. The most productive tuna fishermen were the 'Stick Boats' that would harpoon a few big fish each day in late summer and early fall. In my late teens (after my *Albatross* Deck Hand years) I worked on a private sport fishing boat and we caught 400- to 700-pound tuna on heavy rods and large Penn reels – typically, a three- to four-hour fight per fish. One year we landed fifteen of these monsters before Labor Day but only received five cents per pound 'dressed out' (gutted and with massive head removed). Catching the large fish with rod and reel was just for sport, and beer money for me! Do the math – I received only $45 per fish compared to $5,000 to $20,000 per fish today, for Japanese sushi. The point is, no saltwater limits nor licenses for tuna fishing back in the 1960s!

Needless to say, there were no regulations on the quantity or size of lowly flounder you could bring home from a day's fishing. Local fishermen only saved the largest flounders and threw back the small ones. On most days, a galvanized, fifteen-gallon 'washtub' could be filled with flounders in an afternoon's fishing in the Bay. That's a lot, given each fish is only about one-inch thick!

The unwritten 'size rule' for flounders was very different for Dennis fishermen than for tourists from New York and farther south, who wanted to keep fish that were barely longer than eight inches. Amusing stories on this topic are saved for later in the book.

3

Sesuit Creek and Harbor

Sesuit Creek is a small, natural tidal inlet from Cape Cod Bay, located in East Dennis. The Creek runs southward from the Bay then westward, continuing as a narrow stream through a large saltmarsh before reaching its terminus at Scargo Lake near the center of Dennis village. Sissuit was the original name used by the local Native Americans for the northeast, land portion of Dennis. Nobscusset and Quivet were areas situated to the west and east, respectively, of Sesuit Neck. The term Neck is used to designate a tract of land adjacent to a creek, river or estuary.

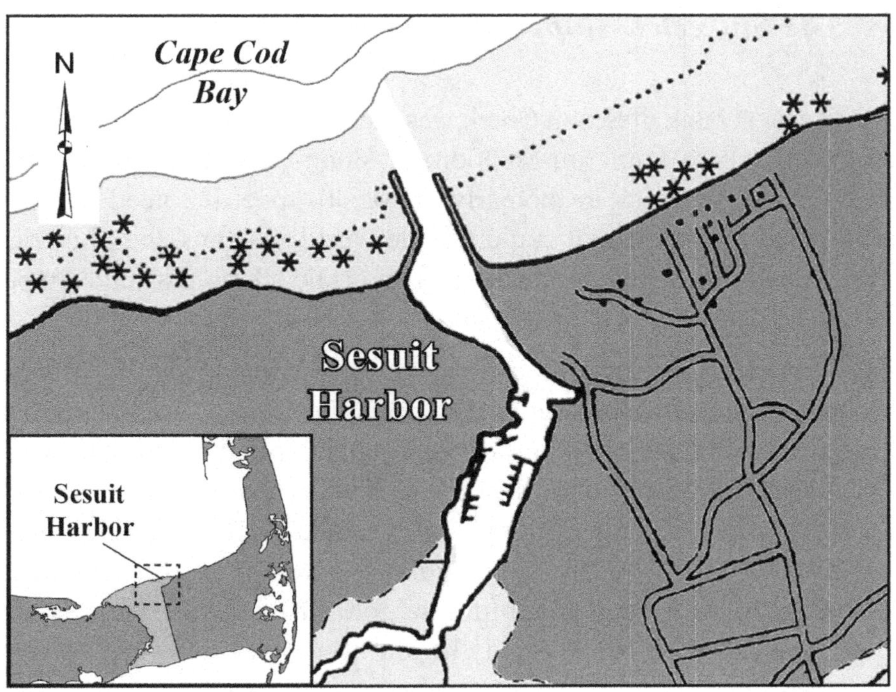

The Shiverick Shipyard – 1800s

The west bank of Sesuit Creek was the original site of the Shiverick Shipyard where numerous schooners, sloops and small brigs were built as fishing boats in the early 1800s. To meet the need for fast-sailing cargo vessels that could ply the world's oceans, the Shiverick yard transitioned into production of majestic, three-masted 'clipper ships'.

Clippers were graceful vessels designed for speed, with long, slender hulls, an overhanging bow and three very tall masts that could support a large sail area. Speed was more important than cargo area for certain commodities, such as the first tea of the season from China, brought to the wealthy in America and England. Clippers also represented relatively fast competition for westward overland travel across America during the California gold rush. Needless to say, the gold business died quickly and clippers were eventually replaced by powered vessels.

The first Shiverick clipper was launched in 1850 and seven others were built over the next fourteen years. All were launched as mostly bare hulls and either towed or crudely sailed to Boston where the masts were stepped and the sail rigging completed.

Five of the clippers were classified as medium-sized; three others were 'extreme' clippers. The largest vessels ranged in length from 150 to 180 ft, which is remarkable given the narrow width of the Creek. Vessel beams were 32 to 38 ft and draft of 20 to 22 ft when fully loaded, but loading did not occur within Sesuit Creek. Tonnage ranged from 550 to 1,200 (versus the 20-ton *Albatross*) with the *Webfoot* having the largest capacity. Because of their deep draft, initial launches were carefully scheduled with the highest tides. The name and year of launch are given below for each of the famous Shiverick clippers:

Revenue	1850
Hippogriffe	1852
Belle of the West	1853
Kit Carson	1854
Wild Hunter	1855
Webfoot	1856
The Christopher Hall	1858
The Ellen Sears	1863

The Shiverick Shipyard gained worldwide notoriety for its sleek clippers during the Golden Age of Sail. Dennis became well known as the only town on Cape Cod where clipper ships were built. The skilled, local Captains and crew also became legends on the high seas.

One story claims that in 1863, two Howes brothers from Dennis met while in the port of Calcutta, India. Captain Allison Howes (a male) was master of the famed clipper *Belle of the West*, whereas Captain Levi Howes was master of the ship *Starlight*. They agreed to race back to their home port of Boston, a distance of roughly 17,000 miles. It ended in a tie which is remarkable as this would have taken 71 days if averaging 10 knots! Typical Dennis boys playing on the high seas.

Note that large clippers often sailed at 14 to 17 knots, with the fastest recorded speed of 22 knots. Many of today's largest cargo and container ships are slowing down to clipper speeds in order to conserve fuel and reduce carbon emissions to the atmosphere. Sea-going progress over 160 years!

Asa Shiverick, the patriarch of the Cape Cod shipbuilding business, died in 1861 at the age of 71. He and most of his family are buried in the Dennis Village Cemetery. A bronze plaque honoring the Shivericks was dedicated in 1924 and can be found on the hill overlooking the west side of the harbor on Sesuit Neck Road. Four roads in Dennis have been named after Shiverick clippers; two others in Yarmouth Port.

Sesuit Harbor Development: 1945 to 1980s

Sesuit Creek was identified as a potential harbor of refuge within Cape Cod Bay as early as the 1940s and plans were developed to deepen the channel and create a turning basin within the Creek. The eastern stone jetty was built in 1945 followed by the two-segment western jetty a few years later. The main entrance channel was deepened to six feet below Mean Low Water and a boat ramp was installed on the west side of the new harbor in 1948.

Ten years later, the Massachusetts Division of Waterways conducted a major dredging project in both the north and south basins to create a larger Sesuit Harbor. Additionally, the main harbor channel was deepened to eight feet below Mean Low Water. This dredging greatly increased the number of mooring locations in the southern portion of the harbor but piers for only a few dozen town-operated boat slips were constructed on the west side. This was a small fraction of the town slips that exist today, on both sides of the harbor.

For the local children at the time of the major 1958 dredging project, the most memorable event was when a large excavator (back-hoe) sunk into the mud near Route 6A in East Dennis. During dredging, mud from the south basin was pumped as a slurry through large pipes to a location in the marsh well inland. A large area of the marsh was covered with the 'dredge spoils' and the brown mud was left exposed to dry. Someone on the construction team made the wrong decision to leave their large digger on the spongy marsh. When the engineers returned a day or two later, they discovered the heavy machine had settled into the marsh about three feet deep and was still sinking. Eventually, the equipment was dug out and recovered but not until hundreds of local folks had gawked and laughed at the site, with photos appearing in the Cape Cod Standard Times.

Following the extensive dredging, Sesuit Harbor was primarily a mooring basin with a small number of town-operated boat slips on the southwestern shore and a single, poorly paved ramp for launching small trailered boats. Locals knew not to back down far at low tide because their trailer's rear wheels would go past the concrete blocks into deep water and big problems would occur with the rising tide.

In those days, money was tight for most Cape Codders. No fancy SUVs with four-wheel drive to pull their boat trailers. Locals had pick-up trucks or maybe an old Willy's Jeep with four-wheel drive. And the parking lot was unpaved; fortunately, no parking fees. More importantly, each boat had only a single, two-stroke outboard engine. Today, some boats have three or four huge, four-stroke outboards. Can you imagine what the old-timers would have said if they'd seen these high-performance vessels backing down the ramp? Surely a snide remark about the owner and a lopsided horsepower-to-brainpower ratio.

Boat traffic in the harbor continually increased from the 1960s into the late 1970s but maintenance dredging of the main channel was not conducted until 1976, by the Massachusetts Division of Waterways. In 1982, the U.S. Army Corps of Engineers (USACE) designated Sesuit as a Harbor of Refuge and authorized periodic maintenance dredging under the distinction of a Federal Navigation Project. From 1982 through 2009, the channel was dredged a total of twenty-one times; five events funded by the Town of Dennis; the remaining sixteen by the USACE.

When annual dredging was postponed, for various reasons, the channel segment between the jetties often became impassible near low tide due to sediment accretion. On a number of occasions, the *Albatross* was used for 'unofficial dredging'. Captain Dave Howes had purposely built the vessel with a protective skeg such that it could sit on the bottom without damaging the shaft, propellers and rudders. This proved invaluable because when the channel filled with sand, Dave and his Father would conduct a brief 'dredging' operation on the outgoing tide to deepen the channel.

With a large anchor set offshore of the shallowest point in the channel, the *Albatross* would anchor in the channel, engines running and with its bow headed inshore so its propwash would erode the bottom sediments and have them carried northward with the outgoing flow. When the channel had achieved the desired depth at that location, ten feet of anchor line would be pulled aboard so the next phase of dredging was conducted a bit farther north (offshore) in the channel. Conducted over most of a six-hour ebb flow period, this dredging operation would result in a significantly better channel for deeper vessels.

In those days, practical solutions were implemented quickly rather than waiting for the next major dredging project to be initiated, sometimes a year later.

A Herring Highway

Schools of Atlantic herring made their annual Spring spawning pilgrimage through Sesuit Creek, from Cape Cod Bay to Scargo Lake. While this creek seemed not to experience the large numbers that transited Quivet Creek a couple miles to the east, many of the eight- to ten-inch river herring would use Sesuit for their life-sustaining return from the sea. In my early teens, I had suspected their only obstacle was my cousin and me using dip nets to catch herring for roe and the dining pleasure of our families. After school near Easter season, we'd come home wet in our hip boots and stinking of fish but our Mothers were forgiving. "Strip down outside!" was their command.

In the early 1960s, the Massachusetts State Fish and Game Department chemically 'shocked' Scargo Lake with rotenone poison to rid all 'nuisance' fish like eels and herring before the first-annual stocking of trout from State fish hatcheries. Rotenone is still widely accepted in the U.S. and elsewhere as a piscicide – a nonselective fish killer. We boys were fascinated by the variety and size of the fish that floated to the surface but none could be eaten due to the poison dispersed into the lake – it seemed a big waste to us young 'subsistence fishermen'.

The First Private Marina in the Harbor

Now, as retired Baby Boomers, we remember the small private dock that existed in the early 1960s, at the present site of Northside Marina on the west side of Sesuit Harbor. The marina was run by "Old Man Lynch" as we kids called him. He was probably in his seventies as we were early teens; he just seemed damn old. He was assisted by his daughter Marie who sold boating supplies, snacks and seaworms for bait. Their small retail store was located at the exact site of today's Sesuit Harbor Café – one of the most popular waterside seafood restaurants in the area.

Marie's husband Wally maintained the small fleet of (maybe four) wooden skiffs that could be rented by the hour. Each skiff had a single five-horsepower outboard engine that was effective for attaining maximum speeds of about ten knots – fast to a young boy alone in the skiff. We were allowed to use the boats for free on days when there was no rental business. Because the outboards were two-stroke gas engines, they used a mixture of gas and oil for fuel and emitted clouds of oil-rich, blue smoke as exhaust – not liked by today's environmentalists! Whenever I smell two-stroke exhaust, I instantly return to my fond memories of fun in the wooden skiffs at Sesuit Harbor.

Wally was the founder of Dennis Equipment Company, now located on Route 134 in South Dennis. Note that Dennis Elders have always been amused that South Dennis is actually located north of Dennis Port and West Dennis, both residing on Nantucket Sound. Whoever established the cartography and village names of this town needed a better compass.

Southward view of Sesuit Harbor

Sesuit Harbor Today

The economy in Dennis certainly has improved over the past fifty years and the boating facilities at Sesuit Harbor are vastly upgraded as well. The Town dock now offers 133 slips on the west side and another 127 on the east, plus excellent double-width boat ramps on both sides. Sewage pump-out stations and fish-cleaning tables add to the health-conscious spirit at the harbor. The situation is so favorable that the demand far exceeds the availability of boat slips at the Town facility and the wait time for a boater to obtain a new slip is 25 to 30 years. And with the Town piers extending far southwestward (up the creek), there is minimal area for moorings compared to the 1960s.

The Northside Marina, a private facility, is running a very successful operation immediately to the north of the Town pier on the west side of the harbor. It offers 120 'wet' slips accommodating boats up to sixty-five feet in length, rack storage capabilities for 150 boats up to twenty-six feet in length and full haul-out and marine repair facilities.

Although Sesuit is primarily a recreational boaters' harbor, there are numerous commercial boating enterprises that operate during summer months from the harbor. These include the fishing vessel *Albatross*, numerous chartered sportfishing boats, sea clam and mussel draggers, a lunch/dinner cruiser called the *Lobster Roll*, a parasailing business, rental boat businesses and likely others that have not been identified here.

Overall, Sesuit Harbor has grown remarkably from its initial dredging in the 1940s. It provides seasonal berthing for over 500 boats plus capabilities for nearly 100 trailered boats daily. An excellent drone overflight of Sesuit Harbor is provided via a link on the website of Northside Marina: http://northsidemarina.com/#foobox-2/0/3Hp6U7qxA5Q

4

Tides and Currents in Cape Cod Bay

The productivity of bottom fishing in Cape Cod Bay varies on all times scales, from decades to minutes. Long-term variations in fish populations may be associated with climate changes, fishery lifecycles and other natural factors. Seasonal and day-to-day variations in fish catch also are observed, likely influenced by local meteorological storms, water temperature fluctuations, variations in suspended sediment concentrations that alter water clarity, plankton productivity cycles, bait availability for the ground fish, natural predation and to a lesser degree, effects of recreational fishing. Note that all of these factors are beyond the control of the *Albatross*' Captain.

By far, the largest problems for ground-fish stocks are commercial fish trawling and clam dragging, both of which are permitted in Cape Cod Bay by the NOAA National Marine Fisheries Service. Bottom trawling for ground-fish wreaks havoc on bottom conditions, often destroying eel grass beds and algal communities which represent essential habitat for small species that are the primary food source for preferred bottom fish (flounder, sea bass, etc.). Even worse are the draggers that tow 'clam dredges' which dig a few inches into the bottom across broad swaths as the heavy equipment is towed behind the dragger. These dredges cause extreme damage to natural bottom habitats and biological communities, which may not reestablish for many years.

Another matter to consider is the much-improved accuracy of vessel navigation with today's GPS positioning systems. In the past, fishing trawlers conducted bottom trawling along compass headings (straight lines) without the ability to keep accurate (+/- 5-ft) records of where they had traveled. Now, GPS navigation systems retain all positions and tracklines such that Captains can see where they have dragged their bottom gear. Parallel trawling lines can be pre-established so the vessel always covers ground never previously visited. The result is that every bit of seafloor is dragged with no undisturbed bottom habitat remaining. If you care about the future of recreational fishing for bottom species in Cape Cod Bay, lobby your politicians to pose increased restrictions on bottom trawling and clam dragging.

Tides

Tides may also have an effect on feeding cycles of bottom fish such as winter flounder. Within the Bay, water levels rise daily due to gravitational forces of the moon, with minor influence from the sun. Two high tides and two low tides occur daily, as driven by the M2 tidal constituent (called the Principal Lunar Semi-Diurnal constituent by oceanographers) that has a period of 12 hours and 25.2 minutes. Thus, high and low tides occur 24 hours and 50 minutes later each day. This is well known by avid beachgoers.

At Sesuit Harbor, the tidal range (height between high and low water) varies between roughly nine and twelve feet, which is large compared to regions south of the Cape having three- to five-foot ranges. Only in the vicinity of Wellfleet Harbor are tidal ranges (slightly) greater than at Dennis. Plymouth and Boston tidal ranges are roughly a foot less than at Sesuit.

It is possible that bottom currents driven by tidal fluctuations can affect the feeding behavior of flounder. In areas having bottom topography, such as a small rise or rough topography, temporarily accelerated tidal currents may resuspend bottom sediments and benthic organisms (e.g., worms and critters that live in the sand/mud) that flounder feed upon. During a twelve-hour tidal cycle, strongest currents occur midway between times of high and low water and these may affect fish activity. Consider this when fishing.

Additionally, tidal currents are further accelerated during 'spring' tides when the relative orientation of the sun, moon and earth cause increased (vertical) tidal ranges. These spring tides occur at roughly fourteen-day intervals, with weaker 'neap' tides occurring between the spring tides. Neap simply pertains to periods when the tidal range is reduced to eight or nine feet compared with twelve feet during spring tides in Cape Cod Bay. Note that avid clammers focus on a few of the highest spring tides each year, but there are many tides with above-average vertical ranges that are also categorized as spring tides.

To understand the tidal flow regime in Cape Cod Bay, it's easiest to imagine looking down on the earth from a satellite perspective. The tide is represented by an actual bulge of water moving counter-clockwise around the upper half of the North Atlantic Ocean. This bulge is what we call 'high water' and it progresses as a wave, moving southward past the Canadian coast then along the New England shore, reaching Boston before entering Cape Cod Bay. Low water follows six hours and twelve minutes after high water, as the water level drops roughly ten feet over this short time period.

Currents

With the incoming tide, water flows into the Bay through its northern, open boundary: an imaginary line seventeen-miles long between Race Point (Provincetown) and Marshfield (north of Plymouth). The incoming current flows southward in the Bay's center, but near the southern boundary of the Bay, from Barnstable to Brewster, the flood current flows eastward, parallel to shore. Maximum tidal current speeds are generally about one knot (1.7 feet per second) with some acceleration during the time of spring tides. Ebb flow north of Dennis is westward and shore-parallel. Consequently, flow offshore

Sesuit Harbor is a simple, bi-directional regime except during storms which can induce wind-driven surface currents in the direction of (technically, somewhat to the right of) winds.

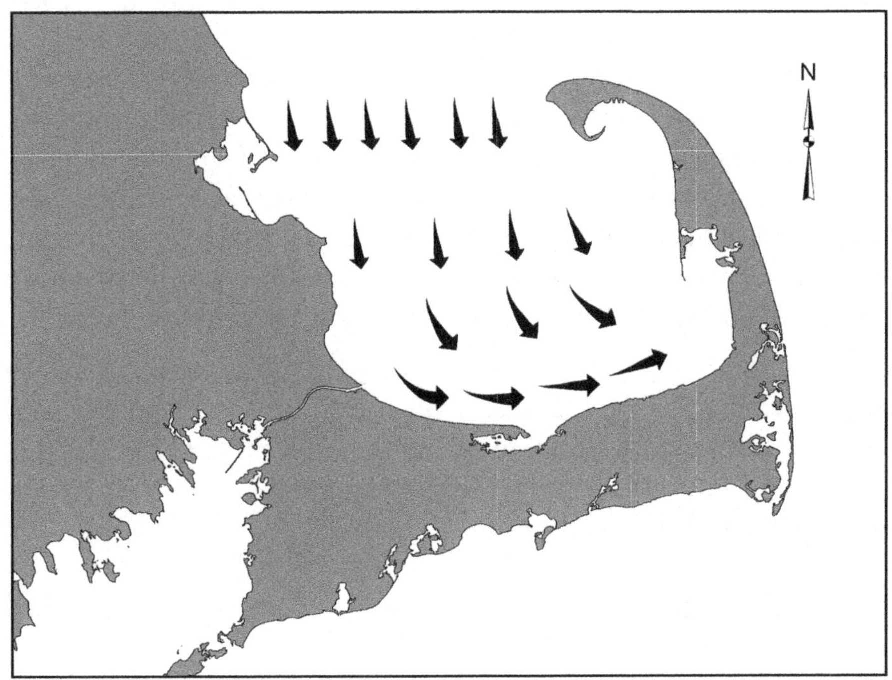

Currents during rising/incoming tide.

The Bay experiences substantial horizontal flow and flushing as driven by the semi-diurnal (twelve-hour) tide. This is why Cape Cod Bay water is relatively cool and clean, with daily supply of water from Massachusetts Bay and the deep, pristine Gulf of Maine. Villagers from towns along the north shore of the Cape are justifiably proud of their clean Bay water.

Just how much flushing is there? The surface area of Cape Cod Bay is 604 square miles. This is twenty-seven times larger than the area of the entire Town of Dennis: 22.3 square miles. If we realize that the whole Bay rises roughly ten feet every six hours, this volume of water would fill Dennis to a height of 270 feet! Certainly, a lot of water flushing the Bay every tidal cycle!

The seventeen-mile long Cape Cod Canal is an interesting man-made feature with very strong tidal currents that attain four to five knots every six hours. However, its small dimensions (480-foot width and 32-foot depth) precludes any major impact on flow in the Bay. Canal tidal currents are associated with the differences in water level between Cape Cod Bay and Buzzards Bay, located at the west end of the Canal. At Sandwich on the east end of the Canal, the vertical tidal range averages ten feet compared to four to five feet at the west end of the Canal. And the times of high and low water are out of phase by three hours at the opposite ends of the Canal. As a result of these water level differences, currents are very intense with only brief periods of no current and slack water when the tidal currents change direction.

Regarding local terminology, eastward flow in the Canal is considered the 'flood' phase as the water is filling Cape Cod Bay when its water level is low. Ebb flow in the Canal (leaving Cape Cod Bay) is oriented westward with speeds exceeding five knots; somewhat stronger than the flood currents.

5

Captain Dave Howes - Original Owner

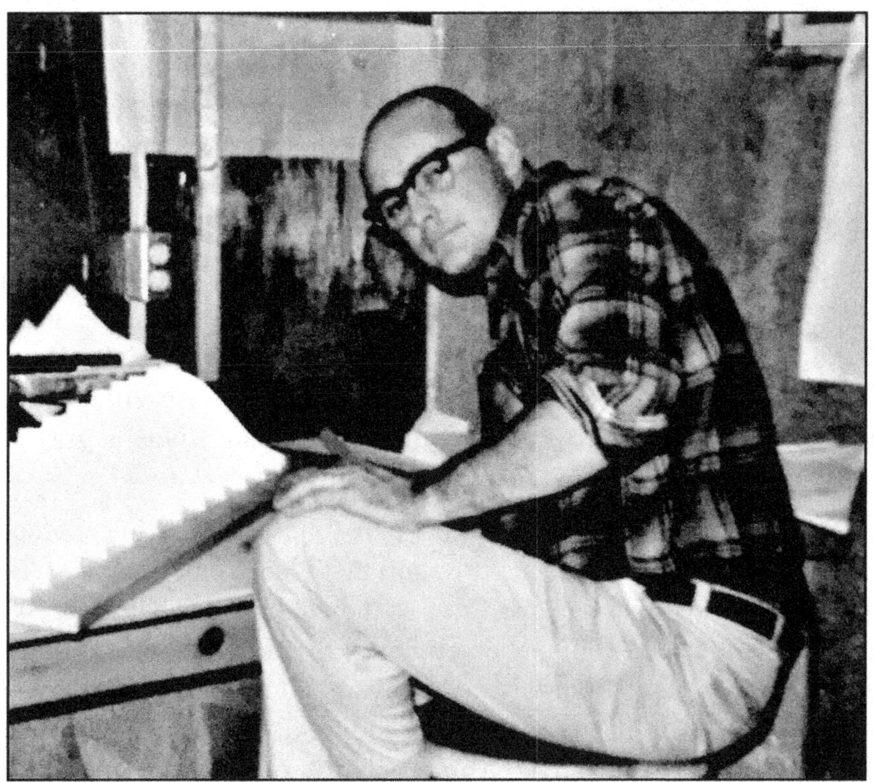

Dennis village has spawned a long list of mariners since its initial settlement in 1639. Being one of the first families to call Dennis its home, the Howes family was deeply entrenched in maritime life and trade. In 1959, nineteen-year-old Dave Howes attended the Massachusetts Maritime Academy. He later graduated from the program with a Third Mate's license as a Merchant Marine Officer upon Oceans, a B.S. degree and a Naval Reserve Commission.

The Maritime Academy was well known by the Howes family. Dave's father Harold, called 'Skip', had graduated thirty years before and enjoyed an interesting career on the sea. While in the Navy, Skip was stationed in Hawaii as a PT Boat skipper and saw action on December 7, 1941. Dave, age 16 months, and his Mother also were there. Later in the war, Skip commanded a 165-foot salvage and rescue vessel in the Caribbean.

Skip and family moved back to Dennis village after the war and he became a school teacher. Dave recalls his Father working hard at two jobs to make ends meet. In those days the town didn't pay teachers very well. "I couldn't look a meatloaf in the face 'til I was about thirty!" meaning it was all too common when growing up.

Skip later became a Marine Surveyor with skills for assessing the seaworthiness and operating systems of all vessel types. He was a founding member of the Society of Marine Surveyors, which today is the National Association of Marine Surveyors. In Dennis village, Skip was remembered as a real 'salt' with a fire-hydrant shape, a gravelly voice and extensive knowledge of seagoing matters.

As a side comment: I worked part-time during winter school vacation throughout my teens. Any job that would pay was ideal. For a while, I worked for Skip and Dave as they built a new home for Skip off Whig Street in Dennis. I remember Skip joking about wanting to construct the kitchen floor with a downward pitch in one direction and put open scuppers in the corners so he could take a hose and wash down the floor like he had done on his boats. For some reason the plan was abandoned and all floors were constructed horizontally.

I had wondered if Skip's 1932 graduating class at the Maritime Academy was its first but Dave assured me it was not. The Academy was founded in 1891 as the Massachusetts Nautical Training School. It remains the oldest continually operating maritime academy in the U.S. Having begun as a floating maritime trade school with initial enrollment of 40 students, training was aboard a school ship berthed next to the USS Constitution in Boston Harbor. In 1913 its name was changed to the Massachusetts Nautical School and finally to its present name in 1942 when the school was moved to Hyannis.

In 1948 the Academy obtained a new training ship, the USS Charleston, a former Navy gunboat. Because its draft exceeded that of Hyannis Harbor, the Academy was relocated to its present location in Buzzards Bay on the Cape Cod Canal.

Dave graduated from the Academy in 1962 at 22 years old. It was a three-year curriculum without summers off; just two-week vacations in summer and winter. There were no girls enrolled in the Academy back in those days.

Captains Dave Howes (right), Chip Carroll (center), Kevin Huck (left)

For several years following graduation, Dave served as Deck Officer on freighters, sailing worldwide. These vessels were configured with below-deck 'cargo holds' that were laboriously filled by stevedores (dockworkers) using large masts and booms. These existed before the development of massive container ships which handle the majority of freight cargo today.

Creating the Albatross Business

Dave was able to accrue sufficient vacation time each year to allow summers off from his sea duty. Being young, ambitious and single, he wondered if it was possible to start a new type of boating business that would appeal to the growing number of summer vacationers in Dennis and the neighboring mid-Cape towns. He saw three new 'charter fishing' boats starting to do well in Sesuit Harbor, taking small groups out fishing for striped bass. "These boats charged a substantial amount for four- or eight-hour trips. I figured some people would be happy if they paid a whole lot less to go out and catch fish they could enjoy eating."

Charter Boats are licensed to carry six or fewer passengers and are normally chartered by a single group of friends. 'Head Boats' (or Party Boats as they are sometimes called) are much larger and licensed to carry more than six passengers; some, up to one hundred passengers, depending upon specific vessel dimensions.

In the summer of 1965, Dave decided to give the flounder fishing business a try. He bought a 'pre-owned' lobster boat, outfitted it for bottom fishing, advertised locally and started the *Albatross* fishing business. His strategy was to attract many tourists who would enjoy taking a boat ride in the Bay and catching some edible fish. He offered less-expensive fishing trips than the Charter Boats. Furthermore, he purposely aimed for the family market and was pleased to let the 'gung-ho Super Sports' pay big bucks to go out on the Charter Boats. He wanted fathers to take out "little Johnny for his first fishing trip. If they caught a few flounders, the kid would be all excited and dad didn't have to shell out major bucks."

Furthermore, Dave didn't want the pressure of having to please the Super Sports each trip, knowing they'd be angry if they didn't catch a boat-load of big stripers. It was much easier to please a dad and little Johnny. And Dave could have nineteen paying passengers aboard per trip.

Finances certainly were tight during the *Albatross'* start-up years. Consistent with his strategy of inexpensive trips for families, Dave charged $5 per adult and $3 per child under 12. This surely was undercutting the local Charter Boats but the two camps kept their cool with only humorous bantering across the adjacent docks when the boats were back in their slips at the end of the day.

Dave and the Charter Boat owners regularly eyed each other's patrons and did the simple math to see who made more money each day. Stronger competition actually grew among the Deck Hands, with those from the Charter Boats proudly showing off the big bass they caught each trip. In jest, we Deck Hands from the *Albatross* would struggle to lift up a flounder, pretending we could barely get it off the deck. Yes, the Charter Boat Deck Hands caught bigger fish and got paid more, plus tips. But we *Albatross* Deck Hands had more fun, less pressure from the clientele and had many hours to flirt with the cute tourist girls who were a captive audience on each trip. Mostly Super Sports would go on the Charter Boats; the teen girls always went fishing with daddy on the *Albatross*.

Dave was careful with his money, as it had to cover boat maintenance, licensing, insurance, vessel operating costs and paying his crew. I remember in spring of 1965 when Dave met with my Father and me to present his 'offer' for the first-ever *Albatross* Deck Hand's job. I was fourteen and surely not accustomed to negotiating a salary. Most importantly, I was excited about going floundering six days per week, no matter how much I would be paid.

Dave drove a hard bargain: "I can pay you $5 for the morning trip but I can't pay that much for the afternoon. I'll give you $3 for the second trip, so you'll make $8 per day." Sounded fine to me, no counter offer made. There are amusing Deck Hand comments about salaries in later chapters.

As the years went on, a few more Charter Boats appeared in Sesuit Harbor but the lines of eager tourists on the *Albatross* dock kept getting longer. Dave bought larger boats and even tried running two boats for five years. All of his strategies seemed to work, aimed at the low-priced fishing trip for happy tourist families.

Careful not to price himself out of the market, Dave was hesitant to increase his 'head price' significantly. He recalls having cautiously increased the per-trip price 50¢ from year to year. Many years later, he dared to increase the rate by a whole dollar! It's amusing today to look back at these low inflation rates during the 1960s and 1970s.

What Meant the Most to Dave

Last summer I scheduled time with Dave to discuss my plan to write this book about the *Albatross*, its history and especially the roughly one-hundred Deck Hands that have worked on the boats since 1965. I had my preconceived ideas about what the book should focus on – the personal side of the fishing business and the Deck Hands. But I chose not to lead the discussion by presenting my plan to Dave. Rather, I asked what meant most to him, as he looked back at this small business that's been running from Sesuit Harbor for over a half century.

"It was all about the kids. That's what I enjoyed most. Thinking back, I was kind of a 'Hard Ass'. It was like Boot Camp for the Deck Hands but fun for the little kids who were passengers. And I've especially enjoyed hearing the success stories of the past Deck Hands."

As one of his early Deck Hands, I totally agreed with his initial statement. He was like a Drill Sergeant giving orders to a naive kid of fourteen. I bit my lip and let him continue without interruption.

"For most of these Deck Hands, it was their first job. They said they'd worked before but it was likely when their mother paid them

$3 to weed the flower garden for a half-hour. When they came to work for me, they had to produce, now! Going to sea in any form has always been a growing, toughening and learning experience for a young man or woman."

Although it had been over ten years since Dave had been managing Deck Hands, he surely hadn't lost his intensity. He continued, "You can't be a softy or they won't learn."

I thought to myself, 'That was an understatement!'

I had worked the prior summer as a 'Golf Pro'. Actually, the part-time job (for $1.35 per hour) was to give out clubs at the miniature golf course in Dennis village next to the Stageway Restaurant (which burned down in the 1970s). It was a very easy job and no one gave me difficult orders, especially not with a gruff military tone. That all changed when I started working for Dave, but I sure had fun helping the passengers catch flounder on the *Albatross*.

Captain Dave really enjoyed teaching the young Deck Hands about nautical skills, safety at sea and especially what not to do, such as "Keep your foot out of the anchor line when it's going over the side. I don't want to have to call your mother and tell her you're on the bottom."

A point of clarification: We kids on the *Albatross* were sometimes called Mates but Dave did not; he correctly called us Deck Hands as he knew the official differences between Mates and Deck Hands. By definition, a Mate is a licensed Deck Officer on a ship who can operate the vessel when the Captain is off duty. In contrast, a Deck Hand is an unlicensed sailor, shortened to 'Hand' on a smaller vessel. Deck Hands perform various duties such as handling lines, assisting with anchoring operations, swabbing the decks, etc. We kids on the *Albatross* surely fit into the Deck Hand category: merely cutting bait, tending to lines, helping tourists and keeping the decks clean. Throughout this book, I refer to us *Albatross* boys (and girls) as Deck Hands.

Another comment from Dave on the *Albatross* Deck Hands' duties: "They didn't like the dirty tasks I sometimes gave them. On one rough fishing trip, some of the tourists 'tossed their cookies' inside the small head (bathroom) and the toilet got all plugged up. When we returned to the harbor, I told the young Deck Hand it was his job to unclog the toilet and mop up the deck. He gave me a look of disbelief until he realized I was serious. I told him it was 'character building'."

Looking back over the decades, Captain Dave was a mentor to some Deck Hands and a father figure to others. A strict boss to most, but someone whose sole intention was to teach the young boys and girls how to work hard and hopefully retain those early skills and strong work ethic as they moved on with their careers. He succeeded in this goal, as expressed by the many Deck Hands who worked for Dave from 1965 to 2005. Their stories and positive experiences are given in later chapters.

Dave's career as a Merchant Marine Officer entailed sea duty from fall to spring each year for over thirty years. His work as Deck Officer involved a wide variety of vessels, including:

- Freighters worldwide
- Commercial tuna boats in the eastern Pacific, with 67 days at sea for each trip.
- Large tankers owned by Mobil Oil Company, with 80 days' work then 45 days off – tough for a marriage!
- Oil tankers along the Pacific Northwest, with runs from Portland, OR to San Francisco.
- Coastal tankers, working for a tug/barge company in New York for 15 years. And Captain on tugs and tankers.

"In the early years, it was 'hard scratchin' to find work, calling shipping companies for weeks to find a trip." But overall, Dave's merchant career was successful. Also, he served in the U.S. Naval Reserve for twenty years and retired as a Lieutenant Commander.

Life is good for Dave now. In our recent meeting, he shared his view of the natural progression for most boaters, starting with a sailboat, then moving to a power boat for convenience. Later, most aging power-boaters transition to a slower, more comfortable power vessel such as the 'gentleman's trawler' configuration. Dave's into the power-boating phase these days, albeit a small boat for lobstering with his past *Osprey* Captain, George. Dave laughs that after power boating, it's typically a wheel chair, then eventually it all ends for the mariner when he has 'bought the farm' – death ashore. But that's certainly not on the near horizon for Dave.

The Albatross Boat Name

Samuel Taylor Coleridge and the *Rime of the Ancient Mariner* (poem of 1798) are not on the minds of young teen boys working on the *Albatross*. Nor was I an exception. Not once during the summer of 1965 did I wonder why Captain Dave had named his sturdy fishing boat the *Albatross*. We cut bait and had fun helping the tourists catch fish.

When I was in my early twenties, working at the Woods Hole Oceanographic Institution, I spent two months at 63-degrees south latitude in the Antarctic Ocean aboard the 212-foot Research Vessel *Chain*. Giant albatross flew around our ship by day, then sat in the water close-by on calm nights. Their massive webbed feet were the size of ping-pong paddles and their bodies were so large they could not get airborne unless there was a significant wind to fly towards. The huge birds were as fascinated with our oceanographic operations and pinging, underwater devices as we were with their size and placid nature. I thought of the fishing boat *Albatross* during those nights in the Antarctic, but was glad she wasn't there floundering in the thirty-foot seas.

Fifty-two years after my first summer's employment on the *Albatross*, the origin of the boat's name came to mind, as I sat on Corporation Beach watching the boat transit to another fishing spot. 'Had Dave named it metaphorically as an omen or defining symbol of a large mistake, e.g., the dead Albatross bird hanging from the neck of the Ancient Mariner – the rotting reminder of his poor decision to kill the bird that had fortunately guided their vessel from the clutches of an Antarctic freeze?' Such an ominous representation for the graceful bird!

I finally had an opportunity to ask Dave when I met with him last year. I posed the big question. "Was there symbolism in your choice of the Albatross as the name of your fishing boat? Can you share the story with me?"

"Hell no, no symbolism. – I just liked the majestic bird. When I sailed across the Pacific during my early days as a Mate, I saw them soaring around our ship. Their ten-foot wingspan was impressive! When I started the fishing business in Sesuit, what better name for a boat?"

That was easy. Nothing profound – no simile for the burden of sin or wrongdoing. It just made sense from a practical standpoint. Actually, I was relieved there was no underlying, negative association with the boat name. *Albatross* it was and always will be. 'Simple as that.

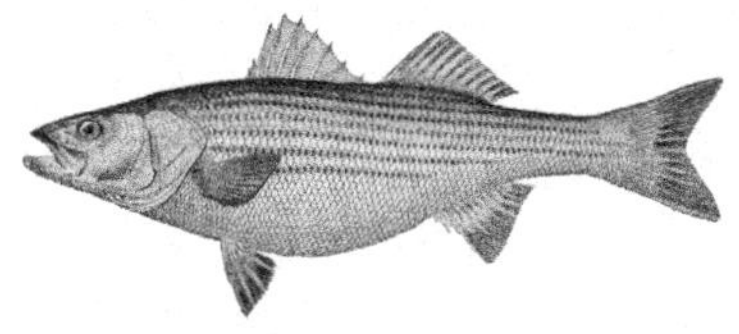

6

Dave's Daughters

Dave has two daughters, Tamsen (Tammie, as she was known on the *Albatross*) born in 1967 and Jennifer three years younger. Tammie was only four years old when the *Albatross III* was built and she still remembers its launch and transit to East Dennis. In fact, the boat and business were a big part of her life from the early 1970s through the early 1990s – twenty years!

I was a Deck Hand the summer of 1967 when Dave's wife brought newborn Tammie down to the boat for the first time. In a recent conversation with Dave, he reminded me that my comment about the small baby was, "We've caught tautog bigger than her." In those days, when I was an early teen and totally focused on fishing, the size of objects was always compared to fish species. "…longer than a dogfish, thinner than a flounder, etc." Tammie's size was distinct as well.

She and I spoke recently and she kindly shared many of her numerous experiences with the *Albatross*. "I did a lot of growing up at Sesuit Harbor. My work on the boat started after school in the spring before the Deck Hands began their full-time summer jobs. My Dad did lots of maintenance and preparations to the *Albatross* in spring; not much in the fall, probably because he'd had enough of the boat and the business from the summer operations. During Middle School years, I helped as a relief Deck Hand during summer, as well as on spring trips when the *Albatross* would take students out for oceanography classes. It was always fun being out on the water each day.

In the early 1980s, my Dad got more business-like with advertising and established a ticket booth in the harbor parking lot. Although I preferred being out on the boat as a Deck Hand, I had to run the booth. At that point in time, having grown up with my Dad, I kind of had his attitude. I wasn't exactly the friendliest person to the tourists but I gradually learned how to be pleasant, which served me well over time."

It was very interesting to hear Tammie align herself with her Dad's personality. I wanted to hear more. "Having spoken to dozens of the past Deck Hands of the *Albatross*, they all said your Dad had taught them a great deal about seamanship and work ethics. But he was tough to work for at times. Was it different for you, as his daughter?"

"It was hard being the daughter especially as I was his first-born. Having worked so many years for him, I can say I know him better than anyone else does. He was a tough guy - if you didn't 'toe the line' for him, you knew it!

There's not a mean bone in his body, he's gruff. He expects people to put out their best effort. To get by that, the motto I had to grow up with was:

Do <u>what</u> you're supposed to do, and

Do it <u>when</u> you're supposed to!"

These words mirror those expressed by another female Deck Hand who worked for Dave, as well as an Alternate Captain, both of whom are described in later chapters.

"My Father has this big, deep, gruff voice and when he says something, he says it with authority. A lot of people take it as yelling but it's truly not."

I asked Tammie about her education and career after stepping away from her *Albatross* duties.

"I really wanted to enroll at the Massachusetts Maritime Academy but my Father, God love him, said 'That's no life for a woman. You're going to settle down and have kids.' So, I went off to become a certified teacher but I didn't do it for long. After having experienced the variety of work associated with the *Albatross* business, I couldn't do the same thing every day. I ended up floating for a number of years, in terms of a career. 'Had a paramedic job, then became a firefighter for a while. Now I'm a Physician's Assistant and enjoy it. I guess the hands-on work with tourists aboard the *Albatross* taught us how to be patient and it prepared us for careers in the public sector."

I have to interject, focusing on Tammie's comment about her 'floating' for a few years. Hell no, she obtained a B.A. in Elementary Education, an M.S. in Environmental Studies and an M.S. in Physician Assistant Studies. Certainly not insignificant accomplishments!

Overall, Tammie's two decades of working with the *Albatross* business were very positive. She did, however, admit that it was tough for her Mom and the entire family during summer months when the boat was in operation. It required 24/7 attention, with the boat, Deck Hands, advertising, phone calls and myriad other responsibilities.

Near the end of our discussion, I asked her if there were any amusing memories that linger with her. She quickly replied that there were so many she didn't know where to begin.

The most amusing occurred on the day of her eighth-grade graduation in Dennis. "It was a spring day and I was committed to helping my Dad paint the bottom of the *Albatross* for the summer season. The procedure started by positioning the boat over the submerged railway next to the town dock. When the tide was fully out, the boat would be high and dry, so we could scrape the bottom. The next rising tide would wash the boat, then we'd start painting on the next falling tide. Because I was small, it was my job to get way underneath and paint in the small spaces between the skegs.

On the morning of my graduation, we began the bottom painting. My wise Mother insisted that Dad slather all my exposed skin with baby oil so the paint would not stick to me. We finished painting just before the tide rose under the hull, and only two hours before my graduation ceremony was to begin.

Mom hosed me down next to the boat then scrubbed all the oil and copper bottom paint from my skin. A quick ride home and a shower, but it didn't leave much time to do my hair and nails! I guess I could handle it better than most girls because by that time in my adolescence I was a real tomboy, and enjoying it.

Looking back, I understand how my personality developed. I saw how much attention my Dad gave to the Deck Hands and that's what I wanted for myself. So, whatever my Dad did, I did it too. Wherever he went, I would go too."

This sounds just like my daughter who loved fishing with me no matter how rough or cold it was. Fathers and daughters.

Jennifer is Tammie's younger sister. Her primary role in the family business was to run the ticket booth, for many years. She had much less time aboard the *Albatross* than did Tammie but shared a similar desire to learn boat handling from her Dad.

Dave described a fond memory of Jennifer on the *Albatross*. "She was to be part of a Girl Scout outing the next week and she asked me if she could steer the boat to impress the other girls. We went to the boat a few times prior to the trip and practiced, with her hands on the helm. On the day of the outing, she took the boat out of the slip, handled the engines and steered out of the channel by herself while I kept a discrete eye on the operation. Needless to say, her stock went up with the other girls.

That learning experience came in handy during a marine salvage job later in the fall when I had to be on deck but could direct her as to how I needed the boat handled. Jennifer was a great help."

It's obvious that the Howes girls have seamanship in their bloodline.

7

History of the *Albatross* Boats

The *Albatross* fishing business began in 1965 and has been ongoing for 52 years as of 2017, with no plans for ending. 1971 was the only year of no fishing operations, during construction of the boat that is still in operation today.

Over the years, Dave Howes named three boats the *Albatross* yet only one has been in operation in any given season. A fourth boat, the *Osprey*, was used in addition to the *Albatross* from 1984 through 1988.

Although the *Albatross* boats were not numbered sequentially (i.e., I, II and III), that designation is used throughout this book to clarify the timeline for operation of each. Descriptions of the four boats involved in the business are given below.

Albatross I

In the spring of 1965, Dave purchased a 'pre-owned' thirty-eight-foot lobster boat having a large aft cockpit and made modifications for its use as a multi-passenger bottom-fishing boat. Coast Guard certification permitted 19 passengers based upon the length of outboard railing around the three-sided cockpit. This boat did not facilitate fishing forward of the wheelhouse which spanned the full beam. Only the Deck Hand would visit the foredeck, to tend the anchor.

The *Albatross I* proved adequate for the first year of the new flounder-fishing business in Sesuit Harbor. That summer, the fishing north of Dennis was excellent and hundreds of happy customers returned to the dock with bags full of edible fish. Only one Deck Hand worked on that boat, me.

Albatross II

Following a success first year, it was apparent that a larger boat would be necessary to meet the growing number of tourists who wanted to participate on four-hour fishing trips in Cape Cod Bay. Often during the summer of 1965, Dave had to turn away customers as he could not exceed the passenger limit of the *Albatross I.*

In 1967 Dave purchased a used Head Boat, forty feet in length, that was originally located in Maine. This boat, hereafter referred to as the *Albatross II*, was better suited for the bottom-fishing business as it had a walk-around configuration that allowed fishing around the entire circumference of the boat. Coast Guard certification allowed 37 passengers fishing on the boat's rail. Dave ran this boat from 1967 to 1970, with the *Albatross* fishing reputation expanding each year.

Albatross III

In 1970 Dave designed a new, larger Head Boat that could accommodate more passengers than the *Albatross II* while incorporating many of its efficient deck features and walk-around capability. The fiberglass hull of the fifty-two-foot *Albatross III* was constructed at a boatyard in Mattapoisett, Massachusetts, and the twin engines were set in place and aligned there. Next, the vessel was towed to Sesuit Harbor where interior construction and outfitting were accomplished.

Dave's father, Skip, installed the wiring and piping components within the vessel. The existing Deck Hand from prior summers, Chris, was employed for months to grind the rough fiberglass from the outside of the hull. Chris later confessed that he would rather have been out floundering in the Bay but it was a paying job and he enjoyed working with Dave and Skip. He vividly remembers the liquid refreshments at the end of the hot summer days in the dusty boat yard.

Dave had a long and sometimes frustrating task obtaining Coast Guard certification for the new vessel, as commercial fiberglass boats were still fairly new to the industry and the Coast Guard was also learning as they went. The entire design/construction project and certification process was accomplished in a little over a year. The Coast Guard approved the boat for up to 49 passengers and the *Albatross III* began fishing operations from Sesuit Harbor in spring of 1972. It has been operating ever since – 45 years and counting.

Osprey

On many weekdays in summer of the early 1980s, there were more eager fishermen than even the *Albatross III* could accommodate. Dave recognized the lost revenue, especially as his summer season was very short; typically, from late June to Labor Day – about 10 weeks. From 1984 to 1988, he ran a second Head Boat, the *Osprey*, to handle the overflow from the *Albatross III*. It too was pre-owned, forty-five feet in length and had full walk-around capabilities. It was licensed to accommodate 39 passengers.

On most days, both boats would make a morning fishing trip but only the *Albatross III* would make the afternoon trip as fewer than 49 customers were typically on the dock waiting at midday. Greg Goolishian was Captain of the *Osprey* for one year and George Machon was Captain for the additional four years of operation. George has shared amusing stories with me about being nervous on his first few fishing trips as the almighty Captain.

One operational challenge that Dave faced was being able to lease only one boat slip at the Town dock. During the evenings, his second boat had to be kept on a mooring in the inner harbor. For the morning fishing trips, Dave would accept passengers aboard the *Albatross III*, head out in the Bay, then George would bring the *Osprey* to the slip for passenger loading. This was quite simple compared to the mid-day choreography.

For the afternoon trip, the *Albatross III* would pull up to the dock, offload morning passengers, get a quick washdown, then accept the afternoon passengers before heading out to the Bay. Next, the *Osprey* would enter the slip to offload its morning patrons after the *Albatross III* had departed.

George was the morning Captain on the *Osprey* and the afternoon Captain of the *Albatross III*, which required him to jump from one boat to the other, just before the *Albatross III* left the dock for the afternoon trip. Dave, the business owner, normally made the decision to stay ashore and have his hired Captain take the *Albatross III* offshore for the afternoon trip. It certainly made for an interesting few minutes when George brought the *Osprey* alongside the *Albatross III*, the two Captains 'jumped ship' and Dave took the *Osprey* out to its mooring until the next morning trip.

After five years of two-boat operations and associated challenges, Dave chose to abandon this cumbersome business approach and opt for use of just the *Albatross III* thereafter.

8

What the *Albatross* Means to the Dennis Community

In 1965, the *Albatross* fishing boat and business had minimal visibility within the community of Dennis village. It was a quiet beginning – a low-profile start-up for sure. There were no street signs, no advertisements at the Drive-In Theater off Route 134, no banners behind planes flying overhead, nor Tweets or Facebook pages to announce the big news in Sesuit Harbor. Dennis was low-key in those days.

Gradually, people noticed the boat in the Bay. It seemed to be out there often. Mostly, it was seen offshore by families spending warm summer days on north-side beaches and by the people who drove into the Town parking lot on the west side of Sesuit Harbor.

As a big marketing push, Captain Dave placed small, black-and-white, paper flyers on the counter of local businesses but they weren't disappearing in droves.

Nor was the *Albatross* a large employer. For the first fifteen years of operation, my three cousins and I grappled onto the 'lucrative' Deck Hand position aboard. Only a few other boys from the village 'got lucky' like us back in those days.

As the 1970s and 1980s passed, the *Albatross* became part of the village lore in summer. You'd hear it mentioned by tourists as they purchased produce at DPM (the Dennis Public Market – Louie Terpos' store, back in those days). And the *Albatross* would often be mentioned when a tourist asked 'What's there to do around here?' in the local package (liquor) store. 'Go fishin on the *Albatross*', would be the standard reply from the guy behind the counter. 'You'll catch a bushel of flounders.' The reputation had begun to gain traction.

In the 1990s and with the turn of the millennium, the tourists' memories of the *Albatross* became fonder and filled with cherished stories. The young boys who had fished with their dads on the *Albatross* were now grown men. They had new families and children who, of course, would love to go fishing like they had done with their dads. And with the dawning of female equality, they had better take their daughters out fishing too – not just a boys' activity. And the girls were determined to catch more fish than their brothers, and they often did.

The tourist wives had heard for years about their husbands' boyhood *Albatross* trips. All the fish they'd landed but also stories of fishhooks in fingers, vomiting potato chips on days of north winds and of the salty, pirate-voiced Captain of the boat. Their husbands had admitted that, when they were boys on a fishing trip, they were jealous of the village boys that became *Albatross* Deck Hands. Now the dads wished their sons could work aboard the boat – the best job for any kid on Cape Cod.

As mentioned earlier, the *Albatross* was a trustworthy timeclock for everyone who sat on Dennis' north-side beaches between mid-June and Labor Day. Monday through Friday, the boat would make two fishing trips per day, typically another on Saturday morning, maybe Sunday morning too if enough paying customers would walk down the dock eager for some floundering. No matter how strongly a few tourists would plead for the boat to leave the dock on a quiet Saturday afternoon, Captain Dave had the final say. The answer was often "No", saying that he had "important maintenance to do on the engines". But us Deck Hands knew he was desperate for time off (and maybe a cold beer ashore). In reality, most of the patrons could return on the next day and the revenue would not be lost.

For morning fishing trips, observant beachgoers knew the *Albatross* would emerge from the Sesuit jetties at 8:40 a.m. and 'head for the barn' at 12:15 p.m. Her bow would re-emerge at 1:10 p.m. then disappear between the jetties at 4:50 p.m. – clockwork.

Those who'd been fishing on the *Albatross* knew how excited the day's patrons were, as the boat headed out for 'deep-sea fishing'

– hearing from the Captain how to bait their hooks, what they'd catch and what to do if they 'caught a whale'. For a kid's first trip on the ocean, it was like visiting the Land of Oz and their faces filled with awe when the Captain spoke about the sea and the fish they would catch.

Each year, vacationing mothers would return to Dennis to relive their favorite moments of years prior. New experiences would be exciting and maybe a new, upscale restaurant would appear in the village, but most wanted to relive their cherished moments each summer, like tasting their favorite ice cream from Smugglers or satisfying their morning donut craving or fried clams for dinner from the seasonal Shacks. Similarly, they wanted to see the *Albatross* plying the seas as they unfolded their beach chairs on their first day in the sun. They didn't want anything to change in Dennis, even their favorite fishing boat.

Scargo Tower in Dennis Village

Vacationing dads would plan at least one fishing trip each week during the family excursion. He'd take his young son or daughter out on the *Albatross* and have them sit on the same bench as where he sat with his dad, thirty years prior.

In August of 2017, a man in his sixties came aboard the *Albatross* for a fishing trip with his young grandson. They had a great morning, with many flounders and black sea bass landed. During the trip, the grandfather explained that it was his grandson's tenth birthday and that he, the grandfather, first went fishing on the *Albatross* on his tenth birthday as well. Both his father and grandfather were part of that event in 1967. Doing the math, the initial grandfather was born around 1907 and fished on the *Albatross* in his sixties. Five generations of this family had now enjoyed fishing aboard the *Albatross*!

9

Captain Chip Carroll

Albatross Business For-Sale in 2005

Since 1965, the *Albatross* has attracted families interested in taking their children out on Cape Cod Bay for a leisurely fishing trip. Like many who reside outside of Massachusetts, the Carroll family greatly enjoyed their summer vacations on the Cape. As their two daughters were growing up, father Charles (Chip) took them out on the *Albatross* for a few trips each summer, which he enjoyed as much as they. The four-hour 'deep-sea' fishing trips on the Bay were safe for the young girls and the flounders and small sharks guaranteed excitement amidst many high-pitched shrieks.

One day in August of 2005, Chip's wife Shawney decided to stay ashore while Father took the girls, nine-year-old Sarah and her twelve-year-old sister, Linnea, out for the afternoon trip on the *Albatross*. When Mom drove to Sesuit Harbor to pick up the family after their fishing trip, the girls ran to her, excited as always. Shawney expected to hear stories of all the fish they caught, squiggly things they had never before seen and maybe about whales that surfaced around the boat, but their first words this day were a big shock to Mom. "Daddy's buying the *Albatross*!"

Young Chip and wife Shawney

It was true, Chip had learned the boat and business were for sale and he immediately wanted it to be his. Looking back, Shawney admits, "The girls were right, we did in fact purchase the boat that winter."

Here's the story from Chip's perspective: "The girls and I were out fishing and it was a wonderful day: good weather offshore Dennis, a nice batch of flounder, constant excitement for the girls and no stress for me. But one thing was a bit troublesome – the Captain was not in the best of moods that afternoon and his Deck Hands were taking the brunt of it."

When Chip had a minute to speak in private with one of the Deck Hands, he learned that the Captain, Dave, was the owner of the *Albatross* business. Chip followed with a casual remark to the Deck Hand, "I'm not sure what this guy is mad about but if I owned this gold mine I'd be happy all the time!"

The Deck Hand responded with, "Well, the gold mine is for sale, do ya want to buy it?"

Today, Chip admits that if the Captain hadn't been in a negative mood that day on August 26, 2005, he (Chip) would not be the owner today.

Soon after, Dave admitted to Chip that he'd been running the boat every summer for forty years and he had gotten tired of the routine. This is not surprising as any business owner would likely feel the same way after all those years. Doing the simple math: forty years times ten weeks of fishing each summer, times roughly eleven trips per week results in 4,400 fishing trips. A long, successful run!

During Dave's most recent years operating the *Albatross* business, he had wisely hired an experienced, full-time Captain so he (Dave) could stay ashore most days. Chip jokes that Dave "had the business running smoothly on 'auto-pilot'. He had someone handling the ticket booth for reservations and tickets sales. He'd visit the boat in the morning then again at noon to help with passenger loading, he'd yell at the Deck Hands for various reasons, then he'd depart until the boat returned at 5 p.m." It all looked easy to Chip.

Dave's final decision to sell the boat was also because he no longer wanted to worry about the possibility of a young fisherman getting seriously injured by a fish hook, which Chip could understand. Chip explained his initial philosophy on how he intended to run the business. "I wanted it to be for family fishing trips. Fun, safe and easy – enjoyment for all. And I decided to pay the Deck Hands well so I could keep good ones around for years. Now my Deck Hands make more money than any other job in the harbor." Some have been working on the *Albatross* for over ten years. That certainly is a testament to fair management and good pay.

Dave had experience with marine operations and salvage, using the boat for various towing and oceanographic projects in the off-season. For this work, he had installed a large towing winch on-deck amidships. When Chip took ownership, he removed the winch and constructed a concession stand for selling refreshments to patrons, which proved to be a considerable success. Different approaches to boat use for sure.

Purchasing the Albatross in 2006

The Carroll family certainly was excited about buying the *Albatross* and establishing it as their own business. Some of Chip's friends did, however, joke that it was his mid-life crisis. "A hell of an expensive Harley!" Chip replied to his jesters.

During the early stages of the purchasing process, Chip was unsure what level of cooperation he'd receive at the local bank when seeking financing for the *Albatross* business. Never having purchased a business, especially a fishing business, he was understandably hesitant during his opening statement that he "wanted to buy a boat". Banks on the Cape hear such requests thousands of times each year so their caution and due diligence can be expected. During the line of questioning, Chip was asked what type of boat. "I'm buying the *Albatross*." These few words instantly changed the atmosphere of the meeting.

The immediate, positive response from the bank manager was "Ok, what do you need?" Quite a relief for Chip, and the financing was established in short order (surely aided by his excellent career in the U.S. Air Force). It was apparent that the *Albatross* was well known and viewed as both a successful and stable business from the bank's standpoint.

As a side note, during many significant moments through the purchasing process, Chip heard a specific song playing in the background. It was Bobby Darin's rendition of "Beyond the Sea" which was released in 1959 and later sung by many other performers since then. To this day, Chip is remined of the *Albatross* purchase whenever he hears this recurring song played.

Chip was an Air Force Reserve pilot who flew 'fighter jets' during his first ten years following graduation from USAF pilot training. The photo on page 43 shows Chip with an F-16 aircraft; the same as the Air Force Thunder Birds. The photo was taken at Luke Air Force base in Arizona where he met and married Shawney. Later in his career, he flew 'heavies' as they're called in military flight circles. In New Jersey he was flying the McDonnell Douglas KC-10 Extender which was the top-of-the-line military tanker and cargo aircraft. It offered increased global mobility for Air Force cargo, military personnel, medical support and aerial refueling. When he retired in 2015 as a Lieutenant Colonel (O-5), he was flying the Lockheed Martin C-5 Galaxy, which is one of the largest military transport aircraft in the world.

Captain Chip in the wheelhouse

Since beginning Air Force active duty as a commissioned officer in 1981, Chip logged more than 6,500 hours flying a variety of heavies. He has flown to more than thirty countries for supply deliveries and humanitarian efforts. "Whether it's delivering ambulances and medical supplies to Hurricane Katrina victims or flying Patriot-missile batteries to NATO allies, I'd be involved." Chip said.

"The best part of flying the heavier airframes is that it doesn't matter what military conflict, natural disaster or humanitarian effort is going on in the world. As a pilot of a C-5, you will be part of it." If anyone wonders whether Captain Carroll can handle problems when they arise on the *Albatross*, they need only to recall his exemplary pilot experience in the Air Force. Manning the helm of a C-5 is much more challenging than steering the 8-knot *Albatross*.

For the civilian's education, the C-5 is 247 feet long with a wingspan of 222 feet and height of 65 feet. Compare this with Boeing's newest and largest passenger aircraft, the 787-8, that is 61 feet shorter and 25 feet narrower than the C-5. Chip flew jets that could each carry cargo equivalent in weight to seven *Albatross* vessels at 40,000 pounds each.

Wife Shawney Runs the Business – 2006 to 2015

Happy Chip and Shawney

Chip took ownership of the *Albatross* business in time for the summer season of 2006 but there was one obstacle and it was substantial! He was committed to working another ten years in the

Air Force Reserve before retirement in 2015. Fortunately, in 2007 he was able to transfer his assignment from New Jersey to Westover Air Force Reserve Base in western Massachusetts but he had to hire a licensed Captain to run the boat and 'ask' his wife run the business while he continued to work full-time for the Air Force Reserve.

Shortly after having settled in his new office at Westover, another officer walked by Chip's office and noticed a photo of the *Albatross* on Chip's shelf. "Is that the *Albatross*, from Cape Cod?" He explained to Chip that he recognized the distinctive profile of the fishing boat from having lived on the Cape for years. He had taken his children fishing on the *Albatross* many times, as his father had done with him, thirty years prior.

"Yes, that's my boat." Chip replied proudly.

There were many aspects of the new business Chip had to be careful about because of his ongoing Air Force Reserve employment and Top-Secret security clearance for handling government-sensitive information. "We had to be completely above board." as Chip explained. One obstacle was that he couldn't hold a liquor license for sales to the general public. He smiles when explaining that his wife had to take on this 'very significant' responsibility. Other security-related challenges cannot be described herein.

For forty years, boaters at Sesuit Harbor were accustomed to seeing Dave Howes handle all aspects of *Albatross* hull preparations and fishing operations. He was easy to recognize from a distance and his gravelly voice was not unlike his father Skip's. Now things were different.

10
Shawney Carroll and Her Daughters

Carroll girls: Sarah (left) and Linnea (right)

As told to me by one of the early Deck Hands who had been working at the harbor in the spring of 2006, Shawney and her daughters arrived one day dressed in nice clothing and accompanied by their small Chihuahua, who later became the *Albatross* mascot. Gossip spread quickly that "Some woman from New Jersey was now running the *Albatross*." Over the next ten years, she encountered many challenges running the operation, in addition to frequent comments from local naysayers.

Shawney was capable of handling many tasks simultaneously because she had been a Master Sergeant in the Air Force when she met Chip in Arizona. She was working in the Health Care department processing medical records for pilots who were required to undergo annual health testing and physicals. Accordingly, she was accustomed to interacting with strong-minded men.

The early years of the *Albatross* business are still vivid in Shawney's memory. "It became obvious that in order to effectively run the business, one of us needed to be at Sesuit Harbor full-time. I opted to quit my job and spend summers in Dennis. I ran the *Albatross* business for ten years until Chip retired from the Air Force Reserve. Did I have a clue what I was getting into? No way! It was and continues to be an adventure."

During the spring of 2006, everyone at the harbor noticed when Shawney and her daughters spent many days beneath the hull of the *Albatross* as it was 'on the hard' (up on blocks) in the parking lot. Grinding and applying toxic bottom paint had not been women's work at Sesuit, except for the hard work of Tammie Howes decades earlier. This certainly earned Shawney and her young girls considerable respect from the many grumpy 'old salts' who thought they had seen it all when it came to boating in Dennis. And Shawney hasn't forgotten the toxic bottom paint that would remain in her hair for weeks.

Fortunately in year-one, the Carrolls were able to hire Captain Kevin Huck who had been running the boat for Dave for the prior two years. He had considerable sea experience from king crab fishing in Alaska as well as fishing in Cape Cod waters. He knew the *Albatross'* machinery and how to fish the Bay. His major contributions to the Carrolls' first few years running the *Albatross* are described in another chapter, below.

Running the *Albatross* business was no small task for Shawney, especially since "It was not her thing. She wasn't into fishing or anything like this." Chip explained.

From the outset, she had supported Chip with his decision to buy the business and she knew it was going to fall on her shoulders but she had no idea what it entailed until the first year got underway. Her responsibilities included:

- Collaborating with the hired Captains
- Hiring and managing the Deck Hands
- Coordinating the shared ticket booth at the harbor
- Maintaining a 24/7 telephone capability for direct calls and reservations
- Arranging for mechanical support when engine or other systems malfunctioned
- Managing fuel, insurance, town slip rental arrangements and many other aspects
- Staying abreast of weather reports, making cancellations for bad weather, etc.
- Purchasing and maintaining the inventory of live bait
- Keeping licenses up to date for boat registration and fishing permits
- Establishing the concession business onboard and keeping it stocked
- Advertising via a website, printed brochures around neighboring towns, etc.

'Hard work, especially for someone who had never before run a boat! And she was a full-time, single parent with Chip away in the Air Force Reserve except for occasional weekend visits to Dennis during the first summer. Starting in 2007, the family resided in Dennis although Chip had to travel to Westover for his Air Force Reserve duties.

Shawney kept the business running smoothly for ten years. The local townsfolk and boaters gained tremendous respect for her strong work ethic and commitment to keeping the business viable for her husband. Her eldest daughter remembers it like this. "Mom acted like she owned the harbor. She yelled at lots of people and we were so embarrassed to be associated with her!" As the daughters grew up, they realized their Mom was demonstrating her strength.

Shawney on bottom-painting day

Most importantly, Shawney was fully appreciated by Chip as she kept his dream alive until he retired. Now he runs the business as the full-time Captain and business manager. Today, Shawney is happy to have no *Albatross* responsibilities and she states this openly whenever the opportunity arises. But her daughters say that as much as Mom doesn't want to run the business, she's still very interested on a daily basis, but tries not to show it. Sarah says that when Chip isn't around, her Mother will ask "How's the boat doing today? How many fish did you catch? How many customers? Is everything going well?"

Sometimes, Shawney can't hold back from asking questions directly to Chip. "Did you see that a storm is coming in tomorrow? Aren't you needing to get more bait today? You're down to only three tubs."

Chip is often amazed at how she still keeps an eye on various business details, even from a few steps back. He asks, "How'd you know we're getting low on bait?"

"I checked the last time I was on the dock." 'Seems that ten years of running the *Albatross* business is not like a mental switch you can turn off. I'll say it again – Shawney is an amazing woman when it comes to running a fishing business.

Truly a Family-Run Business

The Carroll family certainly made a wise decision about acquiring the *Albatross* business, as it helped their children mature, interact with strangers and adults, as well as develop skills that have already steered them toward successful careers.

Not only did the *Albatross* business have a positive effect on the daughters' development, the family atmosphere established by the Carrolls created a comfortable bond between the family and the employed Deck Hands, most of whom were in their mid- and late teens. After the final fishing trip of the day, the Deck Hands would hang around the boat for enjoyment and often go to the Carrolls' home for dinner and friendship. The male Deck Hands were like older brothers for Sarah and Linnea, often protecting their 'sisters'. As the girls got older, the new Deck Hands of similar age often "took a liking to" the girls. Sarah recalls the Deck Hands throwing her off the dock into the harbor water nearly every night after the workday was over. This was definitely a sign of friendship and affection from the teen boys.

With the girls now in their early twenties, they remain close friends with the Deck Hands they've known for ten years. They even go out in a group on Cape Cod summer nights for entertainment. And if any male strangers approach the girls, their 'older brothers' step in for protection; "sometimes obstructional" as Sarah has claimed, with a smile. There is no doubt the Deck Hands are screening the prospective boyfriends.

This friendly working environment and camaraderie established by the Carrolls sounds wonderful but foreign to me, an early Deck Hand on the *Albatross*. Whereas now they're all 'one happy family', we boys in the 1960s and 1970s mostly recall working hard, learning a great deal about seamanship from Dave and making a modest wage. We rarely hung around the boat after the last trip of the day. Nor did Dave; he too wanted to get on with his personal life.

Shawney's feeling about the family-oriented spirit on the *Albatross* is equally positive. "I really love how our boat attracts multiple generations of family members. Kids who fished with their parents forty years ago are now bringing their families fishing on the same boat. It's really wonderful to be able to provide this continuity of Cape Cod fun to these families year after year."

The Daughters

Shawney was quick to tell me that she couldn't have run the *Albatross* business without the tireless efforts of her two daughters. Linnea, the eldest, was only twelve during the first year the Carrolls ran the *Albatross*. "She became a fine boat painter, part-time Deck Hand and manager of the onboard concession stand. As she got older, she sanded and painted the boat each spring between college semesters and worked as a Nurse.

My younger daughter Sarah also helped with sanding, painting and generally doing whatever needed to be done as we prepared the boat." She was only ten during the first fishing season. "Now that I've stepped aside and Chip is managing the boat, Sarah runs all financial aspects of the business, as well as being the accountant of other small businesses based at Sesuit Harbor. She'll soon complete her accounting degree and will surely do well with her career."

When the girls were young, before the family acquired the *Albatross*, Sarah's school teachers would always report that she was very shy. But after Sarah's first year helping Mom with the *Albatross* business, she had matured remarkably. At the parent-teacher meeting following Sarah's first summer on the boat, the teacher asked Chip and Shawney, "What happened to Sarah?" The teacher was amazed at how outgoing Sarah had become, with confidence beyond her years. Linnea's teachers made the same observations about her leap in maturity; all attributable to the *Albatross* business.

At ten, Sarah was answering phones for reservations, giving directions to adults on how to drive to the harbor, etc. She even called 911 from the ticket booth when she saw the tall mast of a trailered sailboat hit a power line.

Being the eldest, Linnea became the manager of the concession stand from its inception. Sales included snacks, liquid refreshments and *Albatross* souvenirs. Her Dad would introduce her to the passengers as the "Concession Goddess" which really embarrassed his daughter. Nevertheless, Dad thought it was funny and continued with the teasing for years, at Linnea's frustration. The bottom line is that he has great respect for her hard work. "To this day, she has probably logged more trips than anyone on the *Albatross* in the Carroll era."

Now twenty-four, Linnea speaks fondly of her many experiences with the *Albatross*. "I've definitely worked more hours on the boat than anyone in our family. The first fishing trip on the boat during year one was a big surprise as my Father hadn't made it clear what our roles were. We just did what was necessary and I became a Deck Hand."

Soon she was proficient at filleting fish but one day she cut her hand severely. "My hand started bleeding really bad and all over the fish on the cutting table. No one wanted their fish after that! I quickly went into the wheelhouse and bandaged it up. I told my Dad it would be OK so we didn't have to end the trip early. Later ashore, I got twelve stitches so it proved to be a bad cut."

She remembers all the diverse types of people that came out on the *Albatross*. "Some were funny but other people actually fought over fish. I became used to the general public because of the boat.

What's funnier is that I met my first boyfriend aboard the *Albatross* and he later broke my heart, on the same boat! First love and first love lost. My parents saw the whole thing and certainly had their opinion.

Both Sarah and I had to answer the phone to take reservations. We were young but amazed at the stupid questions some people would ask." Linnea was only twelve when her phone responsibilities began yet she was giving driving directions to Sesuit Harbor. Now she laughs because it was four years before she could even drive a car. Certainly, a maturity builder for a young girl.

"At twelve I was so excited to go to work at the harbor each day. At times I worked in the ticket booth in the parking lot of the harbor. During the first few years, it was shared by the *Albatross*, other commercial fishing boats and Dennis Parasail & Jet Ski. Most of the girls who worked full-time in the booth were in their mid-twenties and I felt like they were my friends. This was cool at my young age! I felt very grown up. I continued working in the booth through my college years.

Sometimes it was hysterical when people would ask if they could leave things at the booth while they went off parasailing. Dogs were OK but sometimes we ended up babysitting for a while. One time, people left their old grandmother in a hot car so we had to watch her too.

At the end of the summer, all of us booth girls wrote or carved our initials in the wood inside the booth. They were college girls. Some flirted with our male Deck Hands.

Working on the *Albatross* was the best thing I could have done as background for becoming a nurse. I matured into a practical girl older than my age. I grew up physically and mentally behind the concession stand.

Recently, I surprised my new boyfriend who's a commercial fisherman. Early in our relationship he wanted to take me out fishing in the Bay for black seabass, until I told him ‘the fishing season is closed for seabass.’ He sure was surprised with my fishing knowledge.”

Linnea has done well pursuing a career in medicine. She obtained her Masters of Science in Nursing Education and is presently working on her Doctorate of Nursing Practice. She also works in the Cardiac Unit at Cape Cod Community College and teaches nursing classes. Her life goal is to develop an on-line teaching business within the nursing curriculum as well as have a family and work part-time in Urgent Care. Certainly, a mission to help people, and not just fishermen. Thanks Linnea.

11
Additional Hired Captains

In addition to Dave Howes and Chip Carroll, a number of other skilled, licensed Captains have skippered the various *Albatross* boats from the mid-1980s to the present. Their contribution to the continuity of the business is easily underestimated, as there were many days (and even years in Chip's case) when the primary Captains could not take the helm. Experiences of three additional Captains who worked in full-time roles are given below, based upon first-hand discussions with each. Comments about other part-time Captains follow.

Commander Greg Goolishian, U.S. Navy (Retired)

Greg was a typical boy from Dennis village who became a Deck Hand on the *Albatross* and worked summers for five years. Like many others, he started in his early teens with minimal work experience although he had time aboard small skiffs motoring around Sesuit Harbor. His story is extraordinary as it illustrates the mentoring and career guidance given by Dave Howes.

Today, Greg is Master (Captain) of the U.S. Naval Ship *Soderman* (T-AKR 317), a 950-ft cargo and vehicle (roll-on/roll-off) transport ship. She is the largest of the Navy's Military Sealift Command vessels, supporting combat prepositioning activities for the U.S. Army. The *Soderman* transports enough ammunition, food, water, fuel and other supplies to sustain two U.S. Army Heavy Divisions with up to 24,000 personnel for 30 days. At 62,644 tons, this vessel is over 3,000 times heavier than the *Albatross*. She is stationed in the western Pacific and services ports in Guam, Saipan (Northern Mariana Islands), South Korea and Japan.

After obtaining his Third Mate's license from Massachusetts Maritime Academy, Greg worked for one summer as Captain of the *Osprey*. Later he joined the Navy and rose through the ranks, achieving the level of Commander before retiring after twenty years of active duty. Following retirement, he became a commercial Captain for large vessels in the Pacific.

Captain Goolishian with South Korean General

Recently I spoke with Greg about his illustrious maritime career and his memories working for Dave Howes, first as a young Deck Hand then later as a Captain. His words of praise where striking.

"Many of the marine skills that I learned from Dave as a kid, I still use today in my work aboard large ships in the western Pacific. Dave was a maritime academy unto himself. Also, I enjoy passing this knowledge on to young men and women who are early Mates on my vessel. It's exactly the way that Dave taught me. What I learned from him was priceless.

It was the perfect job for a kid – learning basic seamanship skills, boat handling and work ethics. You sure aren't going to learn those hands-on skills at McDonalds or Taco Bell! It couldn't have been any better, lots of fun and I always enjoyed going to work on the *Albatross*.

Back in those days, pay for the Deck Hands was minimal but whether I got paid well or not, the life experience you obtained from the job far outweighed any money I earned, especially for the industry I am in right now. It gave value!

Looking back, it was definitely a learning experience. Most significantly, we learned a strong work ethic that carries on to this day. Practical knowledge of seamanship sunk in. I worked with Dave not only on the *Albatross* but aboard tug boats in the Providence River and earlier, as Captain on the *Osprey* during the first summer after obtaining my license from the Maritime Academy.

For a maritime career, Dave was the ideal mentor although we didn't even know what the word meant as young kids. He had a way of guiding you in the right direction. Keeping you out of trouble and doing the right thing. He steered me toward the Massachusetts Maritime Academy and told me what it was going to be like, giving me tips...and I eventually graduated. Basically, because of Dave I chose the Maritime career path and later a commission in the Navy. He kept pushing me, 'You've got to join the Navy, into the Navy!'

All of his advice was right. The Navy and Merchant Marine operations proved to be a good technical career. I make a substantial salary and with the Navy retirement, I'm very comfortable. A lot of it had to do with Dave Howes."

I asked Greg if he had any funny or cherished memories of his time on the *Albatross* and many sprang forth.

"Back in the mid-70's we could make 25 cents filleting each flounder. This was good money for us kids but often I preferred to ride back to the harbor in the wheelhouse so I could learn more from Dave. I did have scars on my fingers trying to fillet too fast for the money.

I've heard that nowadays, Deck Hands sometimes receive substantial tips from passengers. The biggest tip I ever received was five or six dollars, but times are different now.

Because I needed more money for college (at Massachusetts Maritime) I left the *Albatross* after five years as a Deck Hand, taking a job on the Hy-Line boats in Hyannis. But I stayed good friends with Dave and later went back as a licensed Captain on the *Osprey*.

I also remember being a young kid helping Dave paint the bottom of the *Albatross* each spring. I'd be under the bottom painting frantically as the tide was rising with the boat sitting upon the railway next to the town dock. After a few hours I'd be covered with red, toxic bottom paint and Dave would hose me off.

Dave often used fiberglass to alter or repair the *Albatross*. He'd sometimes joke about people having Silver or Gold Wedding Anniversaries, adding that he had his "Fiberglass Anniversary" with the *Albatross*.

And there were days when I ran the *Osprey* and wanted to position the boat on Dave's favorite fishing spots at the same time that he was running the *Albatross*. We'd get the boats so close that we could practically reach out and touch hands with he and his passengers.

I understand that Dave is retired from the *Albatross* and from his maritime career, but he's still pulling moorings from the bottom of Sesuit Harbor, under contract with the town of Dennis. I worry that he might have an accident as he's getting on in years. 'Don't worry, I've got this worked out.' Dave replied. I don't think he'll ever retire.

I sure appreciate the mentoring and career guidance Dave Howes gave me!"

U.S. Naval Ship Soderman

Captain George Machon

George Machon lived just up the hill from the *Albatross* dock and spent much of his childhood years around the harbor. His adult career as an Elementary School Music Teacher gave him summers off to enjoy boating and collaboration with Dave. In his early thirties, with mentoring and hands-on boat training from Dave, George acquired his Captain's license to aid Dave as Captain of the *Osprey* from 1985 to 1988. Greg Goolishian was the Captain in 1984 then George took over for the remaining four years.

Recently, George shared both interesting and amusing stories with me about his years working for Dave on the various boats. I have placed these in later, relevant chapters rather than present here.

To this day, George expresses nothing but praise for Dave, focused on his mentor's seamanship skills. "He knows more about operating on the water than anyone in the region – a real Merchant Marine Officer. It was also a big part of his humor. One day we were leaving the harbor but there were ducks sitting in the main channel ahead. Dave honked the *Albatross* horn twice and said "two whistles" to signal that he was meeting them starboard to starboard, according to the U.S. Coast Guard's Rules of the Road for vessels passing in channels."

George and Dave are both retired now but during summer they spend considerable time together on the water as best friends. Every second or third day, they head offshore Dennis to pull their lobster pots under recreational permits. "For fun and a good feed." they both admit.

George is also an artist who enjoys painting saltwater fish and local boats. His artwork can be found at Vintage & Vines, located on Route 6A in East Dennis. And he's a musician too, as described in a later section about Sunset Jazz Cruises on the *Albatross*.

Captain Kevin Huck

Prior to coming to Cape Cod, Kevin worked in Alaska, fishing on crab boats. That certainly was tougher duty than working on the *Albatross* in Cape Cod Bay. While the Bay has a few periods of strong northerly winds and rough seas in summer, Kevin's sea experiences in Alaska were much more challenging.

Working for Dave

Near the end of Dave Howes' forty years operating the *Albatross* business, Kevin was hired as a full-time Captain. Dave ran the boat on occasional trips when Kevin had a schedule conflict with his career job as a Yarmouth Fire Captain. As described in the chapter on Captain Chip Carroll, Dave was working on the *Albatross* that day in summer of 2005 when Chip learned that the boat was for sale. Dave's less-than-jolly mood that day was likely because Kevin was not able to run the boat. It's all history now.

I had heard many positive things about Kevin from both Dave and Chip because Kevin also worked nearly full-time for Chip and Shawney for many years before Chip retired from the Air Force Reserve in 2015. When I met Kevin for the first time in August of 2017 to discuss this book and hear first-hand, his experiences on the *Albatross*, he spoke highly of his employers and many other aspects of the business.

"The *Albatross* is a great story. I was happy to have worked on it, and for both owners." He especially enjoyed the family aspect of the tourists that came out fishing. "It's a great trip for dads to take their young kids out fishing while mom goes to the mall.

I really loved how many people would come up to me and say 'My dad took me on this boat when I was a kid. So now I'm taking my kids out on it too.' That was how I met Chip the first time. He was one of many that shared his family's history on the *Albatross*. And Chip came back every year."

Kevin first started working as Captain on the *Albatross* in 2003, as Dave's excitement about running the boat was waning from thirty-eight years of summer operations. "It was a great experience working for Dave. He was very handy and able to keep the boat going by fixing everything himself.

From my days working on commercial boats in Alaska, I knew many guys that could fix things but I never met anyone like Dave – always able to make necessary repairs. Sometimes he and I would work through the night, like replacing the head, so we could make the next fishing trip in the morning.

I never really worked with him on the boat. I was the hired Captain and ran the boat while Dave stayed ashore. He'd come down in the morning with the bait, bark at the kids (Deck Hands) for a few minutes, collect the fares and be off. He wasn't afraid to correct me either, if I did something wrong. Boy, if I ever got hot and heavy on the throttle, he'd chew me out for using up too much fuel. But it made sense as he had to watch the (financial) bottom line.

He was really concerned I might hit one of the small boats in the harbor. Spoken in Dave's terms, 'If you hit one of those plastic footballs, I'm going to have your ass!'"

I too remember that Dave had no love for small, fast, fiberglass (expensive) boats; some days he'd snicker at those "plasto-cruisers". Other Old Salts at the harbor referred to those boats as "drowning machines". Sadly, that name was correct a few times over the years.

"I liked that Dave had rough edges on him. It was part of his charm. He's very up-front with you. Brutally honest, with the attitude, 'Toe the line or get your ass off the boat!'"

Although Kevin said "Dave was gruff" he quickly added that, "He'd give you the shirt off his back. He's been a better friend over the years than I could ever have imagined. If I called for help, he'd be right there. One day I had caught a hook in one of my knuckles and the Deck Hand couldn't get it out. As I was bringing the boat back to the harbor at the end of the trip, I called Dave and asked if he would put the boat back in the slip as my hand was a problem. 'Sure' he said immediately. He was caring but couldn't show it." Kevin added.

The Carroll era

When Chip Carroll was purchasing the *Albatross*, he asked Dave if he would run the boat for the first few years. Dave declined the offer but recommended that Kevin be the full-time Captain based upon his experience with the boat and the overall operation.

Kevin recalls his first season working for the Carrolls. "It was the right time. They brought a different flavor to the *Albatross* operation – definitely a positive thing for the business." But Kevin's schedule certainly was demanding. He worked as a fireman on night duty then would go directly to the *Albatross* at 7:30 a.m. to prepare for the first trip. Shawney had to make sure the Deck Hands were preparing the boat, bait supply and other aspects, in addition to loading passengers, collecting fares, etc. Sometimes after the second *Albatross* trip of the day, Kevin had to go directly to his part-time paramedic job at a Coast Guard clinic. He was certainly a busy guy.

"And I couldn't have done it without Shawney's support. I was a single parent at the time and she'd help by shuttling my son to and from summer camp, bringing me lunch on the boat and even doing my laundry! That woman deserved a medal, especially dealing with my madness!

The Carrolls were wise about making much needed upgrades to the boat. They added an anchor winch to save the backs of the Deck Hands, especially for the girls who wanted to master all duties as Deck Hands. They also made the major investment of replacing the two main engines.

At one point, I spoke with Chip about the boat getting old and that it might be wise to replace it rather than sinking more money into this boat. He disagreed, being a bit of a 'boat romantic', and insisted on keeping the original *Albatross* rather than changing the whole spirit of the operation. He believed that a new boat would feel different for his clientele who had been fishing on the original boat for generations.

Chip certainly knew, from personal experience. And the long-standing customers would prefer the exact same boat they first went fishing on when they were kids." So it is, the existing *Albatross* is half way through its fifth decade of fishing offshore Dennis.

In addition to their positive energy, the Carrolls also brought new business ideas aboard the *Albatross*. For convenience, patrons could now use credit cards for ticket purchase aboard the boat. "In the past, some people had actually missed the boat while searching for an ATM to acquire cash." Printing of *Albatross* t-shirts and hoodies also proved to be a lucrative activity from Kevin's perspective and good advertising too.

"The Carrolls also branched out to other activities aboard the *Albatross*. Weekly cruises for the Audubon Society, Sunset Jazz Cruises and Scattering of Ashes Ceremonies all became popular activities and more trips for Captains and Deck Hands. All positive."

Aside from all these business aspects, Kevin most enjoyed the fact that Chip loved owning the boat and wanted it to be used for pleasurable things when not running fishing trips. "We'd all be tired at the end of the week and on Friday nights we were ready to get off the boat and head home. Sometimes Chip would come down the dock following a two-week stint of Air Force Reserve duty and he'd want to immediately take the boat out for swimming and a sunset cruise with the family. It was great to see him enjoy the boat like that! And he still does."

Kevin's view of the Deck Hands

"Dave did all the hiring of Deck Hands when I was Captain during his ownership, so I never knew what I was going to get. Some went on to develop great careers, some others were just 'hangers-on'.

My first two Deck Hands were very young. They'd do anything I asked but obvious things didn't occur to them. It was funny how they'd walk over a hazardous line on deck ten times rather than pick it up but when I asked them, they'd do it immediately.

Because they were naïve, it was easy to play practical jokes on the young ones. I once sent a new Deck Hand over to the nearby marina to buy a 'can of prop wash'." Experienced seamen know that prop wash is the turbulence in the wake of a moving boat but Kevin got a kick out of sending the Deck Hand off to buy what the kid thought was a jug of cleaning liquid.

I also remember Dave trying to pull similar jokes on me and other Deck Hands, when we were in our early teens. He told us to go below and get the can of 'relative bearing grease'. We'd look around the engine room for a while then we'd hear him break out laughing, at us. Relative bearings are navigation sightings based upon compass headings; they're definitely not mechanical components like ball bearings that sometimes need lubrication with petroleum grease.

Kevin continued, describing his guidance to Deck Hands. "I always tried to instill good communication skills in the Deck Hands. 'Go out of your way to help people on the boat. It'll pay dividends. Even if they're not catching fish, chat them up. Where are they from, what do they do? But don't be too obvious with the daughters!

Things have changed over the years, also with proper public behavior by the Deck Hands. In the early days, they'd brutalize the sharks with all the tourists watching but now they have to be more environmentally correct and release them without major harm and gore.

The Captains certainly were a positive influence on the kids. The boys had good heads on their shoulders and turned into successful men. Many have developed fine maritime careers." Kevin definitely enjoyed his days working on the *Albatross*.

Other Hired Captains

Roughly a half-dozen other licensed Captains have operated the *Albatross* vessels for Dave and Chip. These Captains have and continue to provide much needed assistance when the primary Captains could not man the helm. Their good work was and continues to be much appreciated.

I have not had the opportunity to meet with the additional Captains, but stories have been passed along over the years. A couple of the most colorful and easy to remember are given below.

One of the relief Captains thought it was bad luck to have bananas onboard a boat. Superstitions are permissible but this guy took it a bit far. Whenever he came aboard as the relief Captain, he'd throw the sunscreen container of the primary Captain over the side of the boat because it was printed with the manufacturer's name, Banana Boat.

There are many theories of why people believe bananas are bad luck on a boat. One pertains to boats being unable to catch fish when they had bananas aboard. The belief stems back to the 1700s when sailing vessels had to cross the oceans quickly when they had banana cargo. Apparently, the high sailing speed was not good for fish trolling. Another superstition said that bananas would cause a boat to sink – because many boats that had not reached their destination were carrying bananas. A bit far-fetched, given that storms likely were the culprit.

A different relief Captain on the *Albatross* was strongly averse to getting his feet wet! Was this based upon another superstition? Nothing could be found to link this dislike with a nautical superstition or bad luck, but many others exist, including the following:

Nautical superstitions

- Don't step aboard a vessel with your left foot first; the left side of anything is sinister
- Do bring cats aboard as they eliminate pests
- Red skies in morning: sailors take warning
- Don't sail with redheads or people with blue eyes; the vengeful ocean will bring peril
- Pierce an ear so your eyesight is better in the opposite eye; pirates do one ear only
- Don't injure or kill sea birds, especially an albatross; they'll come back to haunt
- If you're becalmed, throw a coin in the sea; it'll buy you wind
- Pay your back bills, as debtors bring bad storms to a vessel
- Don't save a crewmember from drowning because a sea god could sink the whole vessel

12

Male Deck Hands

The Early Years

Back in the 1960s, the Sesuit Harbor neighborhood was a ripe playground for mischievous boys from the village. Simple fun could be had outdoors and on Cape Cod Bay; we needed no instruction nor video games nor I-phones.

As mid-teens, we often joked about the three types of boys who took to the local waters on summer days: Yacht Club boys, Charter Boat boys and us *Albatross* boys. The Yacht Club boys in the 1960s were very different from us *Albatross* boys. Most lived off-Cape in winter, they didn't have to work summer jobs, they wore nice clothes and deck shoes, and most had braces on their teeth. When the weather was nice, they sailed small fiberglass sloops – Rhodes and Cat boats, rarely leaving the safe waters of the harbor.

Next were the 'Chaata' Boat boys who worked on the chartered sportfishing fleet that carried up to six paying customers per trip for striper fishing in the Bay. In the 1960s there were no bluefish in the Bay so only stripers were landed, often dozens of big 'cows' over forty pounds each; 'linesiders' some people called them.

Last but not least, were the *Albatross* boys. Our pay was low (an opinion expressed by many Deck Hands of yesteryear) but we sure had fun. We didn't dress well, typically in tattered, cut-off jeans, bare feet and no shirt – our work uniform back in those days. Certainly, no shirts with the *Albatross* name stenciled on professionally.

Only the Yacht Club boys would wear sunblock and white zinc cream on their noses and lips. As this predated nationwide skin-cancer concerns, maybe their moms were 'smaaata' than our moms when it came to skin care but we didn't know any better.

We *Albatross* boys were all natural and throwing raw quahogs at each other was normal play. We spoke crudely and like most Cape boys, we added 'Rs' to words when we shouldn't, i.e., idea(r), and dropped the R from other words like 'cold beea' and 'haaba', where the *Albatross* was berthed.

We loved to pull pranks on the tourists and sometimes on each other. Stories are plentiful from the Deck Hands, as you'll read below in a separate chapter.

We also enjoyed the rich tourist girls who would visit the Cape from New York and New Jersey, as well as the cute French-Canadian girls with their accents. They were far worldlier than us *Albatross* boys but they enjoyed our crudeness and tanned bodies, especially when their parents would let them meet us on warm summer nights. The Yacht Club boys were totally unaware of the fun we had on the *Albatross*. They were probably having their own fun, within the white walls of their Club.

The Charter Boat boys earned a good paycheck plus significant tips when the fishing was productive but they didn't have lots of girls aboard like we did. Never would we reveal our jealousy of the big stripers the Charter Boat boys brought ashore. Our bushels of flounders were good enough for us. We'd watch the Charter boys lift up their big bass to show off, so in retaliation, we'd lift one of our two-pound flounders, pretending it was so heavy we could barely get if off the deck. Funny teen humor at the time.

Back in the 'old days', Dennis was a modest village from a financial standpoint and Dave was trying to get his business off the ground, with a very narrow profit margin. We local kids grew up amidst the post-war, often frugal attitude of our parents and grandparents. Most folks were happy just to have a single-family home, a yard to mow and a ten-year old car. Now, many village houses are valued well over one million dollars (even those far from the shore) and nearly everyone has a new car. And people have money to put substantial tips into the hands of Deck Hands on fishing boats.

Boys to Men

Many of the *Albatross* boys felt they made the transition from 'boys to men' during the first summer they worked under Dave's orders. The duties included having to regularly pull up the *Albatross* anchor, often five times each trip – about 50 times each week – 500 times each summer. It felt like work at the time but it sure beat washing dishes in a restaurant on a hot summer night. And it got us in top physical shape; much needed for our after-work waterskiing in the Bay.

During the first few years, the *Albatross* didn't have a winch to pull up the anchor. Normal procedure was for Dave to move forward slowly until the bow was directly over the anchor and all the slack in the line was brought aboard. Then the Deck Hand would pull upward on the heavy line until the anchor could be lifted over the pulpit and aboard. Sometimes the flukes of the anchor would be filled with seaweed or line from lobster pots could be entangled, causing the lifting to be twice as hard as normal. The Deck Hand knew something was wrong but Dave's order from the helm was the same – "get the damn thing aboard". For Deck Hands that were as young as twelve to fourteen years old, this could be very difficult. And this surely prevented girls from becoming Deck Hands during the early years of the *Albatross* operations.

My cousin Daniel vividly remembers working as Deck Hand on the *Osprey*, with George Machon as Captain. One day, Daniel started to pull up the anchor as they were positioned north of Barnstable Harbor channel, but the weight on the line seemed much greater than normal. With very hard lifting, he eventually got it to the surface and could see that something else was tangled with the *Osprey's* anchor. It was a shell-encrusted, four-foot-tall anchor that must have been lost from a schooner in the 1800s. Twelve-year old Daniel certainly proved he had a strong back to get that weight to the surface! He still remembers that day and proudly shows the photo of the anchor at Sesuit with he and George, which was published in the Cape Cod Standard Times.

Anchor-hauling terminology

The many Deck Hands who worked for Dave learned hands-on seamanship skills as well as a nautical vocabulary from his employment on large merchant ships during winter months. Not all of the vocabulary was pertinent on the *Albatross* but we liked learning new words that would make us sound like experienced seamen when we spoke to our friends and family. In teen minds, we thought it made us cool and pirate-like (as Dave's voice sounded to us).

For decades, a large winch had been installed on the main deck of the *Albatross III* for pulling in objects astern of the vessel. Dave would take on marine salvage jobs after the summer fishing season. Some of the winch and associated terminology is explained below; useful when you have conversations with seamen and pirates.

- Winch – a mechanical device with a cylindrical drum, around which line or chain is wrapped for hauling or paying out
- Capstan or 'working head' – a winch with the axle of the drum oriented vertically
- Windlass – a winch that is used primarily for anchor hauling, with the axle of the drum normally oriented horizontally
- Bitter end – the end of the anchor line or chain, attached to the vessel. This actually was the origin of this term, that now is used for many topics.
- Chain locker – where the anchor line or chain is stored below deck
- Warping head or drum – a wheel on a windlass that is used for handling line
- Gypsy – a different wheel on a windlass, designed to engage individual links of chain
- Wildcat – the name commonly used in North America for a winch (not wench) gypsy

Deck Hands of Recent Years

The Carroll era of *Albatross* ownership is much different than the prior forty years, as described in a previous chapter on Captain Chip Carroll. Much higher income for Deck Hands and the family-run business environment are the two reasons why most Deck Hands now stick around for many years. Whereas in the early years, Deck Hands were young and typically moved on after a few years, Deck Hands today generally range in age from late teens to mid-twenties; some even older. They can acquire better income than from most other summer jobs and they enjoy being out on the Bay aboard a fishing boat.

Many of the Deck Hands have openly expressed that their dream would be to purchase the *Albatross* when they are old enough to acquire sufficient funds. These guys want to remain Deck Hands indefinitely, seeking other employment during the off-season of the *Albatross*.

One excellent, existing Deck Hand was very bold by announcing that he intends to marry one of Chip's daughters to assure that he will someday own the boat, even if he later divorces her. He said he was just kidding but we think not.

How Many Deck Hands Since the Beginning?

Dave Howes and Chip Carroll each provided me with a list of male and female Deck Hands who had worked for them aboard the *Albatross*. The combined list included eighty names but there have been additional Deck Hands who had worked aboard the vessels over the years.

Dave ran the three *Albatross* boats (one at a time) from 1965 to 2005, minus one year when the *Albatross III* was being constructed, which totals 39 years of fishing operations. In 1965 only one Deck Hand worked aboard the small, 19-passenger boat, and that was Yours

Truly. All the other years required two Deck Hands on each fishing trip due to the larger number of passengers. Some years, there were relief Deck Hands while others were replaced mid-season, adding to the number of individuals who worked for Dave. Also, the *Osprey* ran from 1984 to 1988, requiring two Deck Hands aboard, plus some replacements during those years.

Over the 39 years of Dave's operations, we estimate between 70 and 80 Deck Hands worked aboard the *Albatross*.

Chip and Shawney have run the *Albatross* from 2006 through 2017, using two Deck Hands per trip (not counting the Concession Goddess). During that period, Deck Hands worked an average of four years, with one having been aboard for twelve years. Others worked seldom or on evening cruises only. Twenty-two Deck Hands were on Chip's list provided to me but there were likely others unintentionally omitted.

Thus, approximately 100 Deck Hands worked on the various *Albatross* boats since 1965. A list is provided at the back of this book and will be updated periodically as more names come forth. My goal is to make contact with each Deck Hand to hear their first-hand experiences aboard the *Albatross*. Additionally, I would like to compile the demographics of all Deck Hands, including careers, maritime experience, fishing interests, etc. As new information is acquired, I will publish a revision to this book, likely in 2020.

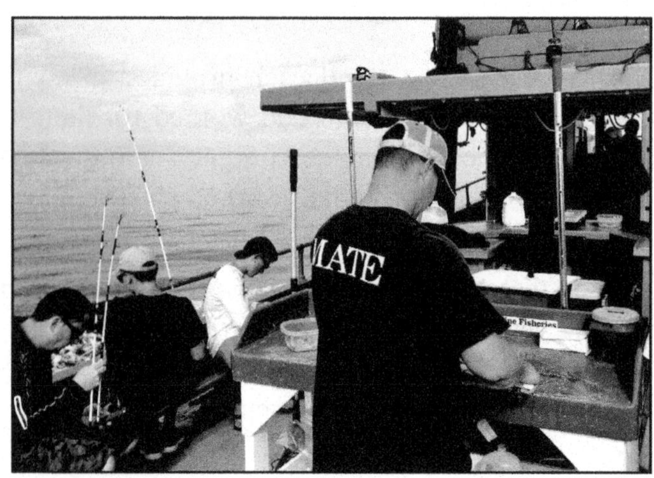

13

Female Deck Hands

Over the first fifty-two years of *Albatross* fishing, all but a handful of the Deck Hands have been boys or men. Despite the small number of female Deck Hands, they proved to be brave, especially during their pursuit of the job that had a male, almost macho, reputation. Given below are two examples of female Deck Hands, starting with Cait who was the first girl 'officially' hired as a Deck Hand by Dave Howes. Some years later, Amanda worked as a Deck Hand during the Carroll era of *Albatross* ownership. Both girls epitomize determination as well as terrific examples of girls' success on a special fishing boat.

Above, in the chapter on Dave's Daughters, Tammie and Jennifer Howes were introduced. Tammie was actively involved with the *Albatross* business for twenty years, with considerable time as Deck Hand. Dave admitted "I always wished I had Tammie as a full-time Deck Hand because she was a 'Cracker Jack'", meaning a skilled expert.

Linnea and Sarah Carroll, the two daughters of Chip and Shawney, also have performed as Deck Hands on many fishing trips aboard the *Albatross* since 2006. Although not formally hired into that role, being daughters of the Captain implied they would do as told, whether it be cutting bait, helping patrons with fishing, untangling lines, filleting fish or running the concession stand. They knew the Deck Hand job as well as any of the guys.

Interestingly, Tammie, Cait, Amanda and Linnea have all pursued medical careers and each have succeeded. It appears that their early experience aiding passengers of all ages on the *Albatross* contributed to their desire to help others through medical careers. Each of these ladies agree with this premise.

Cait – Female Deck Hand during Captain Dave's era

In 2002, Captain Dave Howes hired Cait, his first full-time, female Deck Hand after having run the *Albatross* for thirty-seven years. Dave's daughter Tammie had been a part-time Deck Hand for many years (from the 1970s to the 1990s) but Cait was the first female job applicant since Tammie. In the minds of many past Deck Hands and people who knew Dave well, this was an extraordinary event – Dave actually hiring a girl! Cait had summered in Dennis with her parents and had been fishing on the *Albatross* a few times, but she had no experience working on boats. It seemed like a disaster in the making.

As a little background, Cait admits that her freshman year in college hadn't gone well from an academic standpoint. She wasn't sure if she'd even return to school in the fall. When the summer recess began, she was carrying lots of uncertainty and lack of confidence.

Despite having no restaurant experience, she obtained a waitress job in one of the Cape's premier restaurants but failed miserably and was quickly laid off. "I was probably the worst server ever!" Now she laughs about it but at the time is was demoralizing.

What next? "I really felt like doing something that was a challenge for me, and succeeding! It was a big deal for me to make a change and build my confidence."

One of the Gilrein boys who lived next door in Cait's Dennis neighborhood was an active Deck Hand on the *Albatross* so she knew about his job on the fishing boat. While talking to him about her lay-off from the restaurant, she expressed her urgent need for a summer job. "I don't know what possessed me to say I wanted to work on the *Albatross*, but I loved being out on the water fishing." The next day, the Deck Hand friend recommended her to Captain Dave. To everyone's surprise, Dave decided to give her a one-week trial. "It was a big deal for him to give me the opportunity."

Her Mother couldn't understand why Cait would want this job on a boat, knowing her lack of experience. And Cait admits that her Mother's view was realistic. "I didn't grow up on the water so I definitely had to be shown the ropes, by the other Deck Hand and the Captain. The first week was tough but I loved it!

I think I did OK for Dave because he was a lot like my Dad, who was in the Army and ran our household like he was still on active duty. Dave wasn't overly tough; just very strict – definitely not a 'warm and fuzzy' kind of guy. He wanted things done a certain way. If you didn't do it right, he was very gruff but if you worked within the rules, everything was cool."

Cait must have performed well because Dave kept her on for the remainder of the summer. "It was a great job. I can't imagine any girl not loving it. Dave might have been a little easier on me than male Deck Hands but I definitely had to perform." I suspect she was more mature than most of the early teen, male Deck Hands that Dave had employed, which helped her understand what to do and what not to do. She was eighteen and the other (boy) Deck Hand was only fourteen.

Knowing that most of the male *Albatross* Deck Hands have memories of pranks they pulled on tourists or each other, I asked Kate if she too clowned around at all. To my surprise, nothing came to mind and she added, "I guess I was focused on not screwing up." 'Sounds like wise maturity in the work place, especially with Dave watching over deck operations.

"I loved filleting the fish and the tips were good too." Cait recalls. "Working outside all summer was fantastic."

Her Mother's most vivid memory was when Cait returned from one of her first days working aboard the *Albatross*. "She came home after learning how to clean the fish. She was so excited, and of course smelly, because she was fascinated with the structure of the fish and how to cut it perfectly for fillets. I really believe that was what led her into medicine. She was studying molecular biology in her first year at Princeton but wasn't sure what she'd do with it. After the *Albatross* summer job, she did some research involving surgery on rat brains and she was on her path to becoming a doctor."

Cait loved being a Deck Hand and fondly remembers many elements, both significant and amusing. For example, many of the families enjoyed seeing Cait perform well, as it demonstrated to their young daughters that girls can succeed in outdoor jobs that are typically associated with boys. "Being a female Deck Hand was somewhat of a novelty." As her proficiency in fishing and filleting improved, she enjoyed the respect that came with it.

A fear that she initially brought to the job was becoming seasick, especially since she had always been prone to car sickness. Fortunately, she was 'overtaken with green' only once but she learned to tough it out and do her job rather than 'toss her cookies' from the rail, like the landlubbers.

Quite often, the fishermen caught eels and any Asians aboard were all excited having landed their favorite delicacy for sushi and stew. Not the Deck Hands – they wanted to release the slimy buggers as quickly as possible. Today eels, sushi and monkfish are some of Cait's favorite bites but in those days, they all were considered trash fish.

Political Correctness had not yet entered the fishing world in 2002. Here's a relevant example aboard the *Albatross*. Dogfish were a real nuisance for Deck Hands starting in mid-summer when the waters of Cape Cod Bay warmed up. These fish are notorious for circling when hooked near the bottom. Within a minute they would encircle all the neighboring lines before coming to the surface in a ball of flailing hooks. Consequently, you have ten eager fishermen pulling hard on the same fish, all thinking they've caught a big one! The Deck Hands hate this fiasco and eventually take out their frustration on the dogfish when it's finally free of all hooks. Male Deck Hands would aggressively destroy the fish in one way or another. Cait remembers, "We clubbed them with baseball bats before throwing them back in the water, to the horror of the families and children."

I recall much worse (gruesome) treatment of the dogfish during my early years as a Deck Hand but I will refrain from the descriptions. Cait ended by saying "You did what you had to do at the time. It would be different now."

Cait acknowledges that being a Deck Hand on the *Albatross* was a great job for gaining maturity. "Dealing with people of all ages and keeping a good attitude. And working in that wonderful environment didn't make it terribly difficult."

I recognized a common theme throughout my discussions with many Deck Hands. Although most were younger than sixteen, they were constantly giving instructions to children and adults, on boating safety, fishing and even fish species. How better to mature as an early teen? And working with people from all walks of life and geographies certainly broadened a Deck Hand's world, especially for a boy from Dennis village.

Changing topics, Cait's biggest challenge was the task of pulling up the anchor at the bow of the *Albatross*. There was a small winch to do the main lifting but the Deck Hand needed strength to keep the line tight on the winch and to pull the anchor into its secure position at the end of the process. Although she was a 'girl', the other (boy) Deck Hand didn't demonstrate chivalry; not surprising as he was only fourteen.

"When it came to the anchor task, we took equal turns. I was only eighteen and not terribly strong. I had to psych myself up when it was my turn to pull the anchor. 'I'm going to do it. I'm not going to get my hands caught in the winch!' It was so hard in the beginning but it became second-nature after a while. 'I did it!' It was a BIG turning point for me and Dave saw that I could do the job."

For the remainder of the summer, Cait kept building confidence like never before. She even made up her mind that she'd return to college and *Succeed*. Shortly after being back at Princeton, she boldly decided to get a small tattoo on her back to forever remind herself of her *Albatross* accomplishment and that it was a huge turning point in her life. Not surprisingly, the tattoo was an anchor! Her Mother didn't find out for two years but was initially furious; later she understood the significance and acquiesced.

Being void of 'ink' myself, I did a little reading on the subject of tattoos and learned they can be simply pictorial, purely decorative without meaning, or symbolic with a specific meaning for the wearer. Tattoos can serve as rites of passage, marks of status and decorations of bravery. All of these words accurately depict the significance of Cait's anchor tattoo.

Her summer on the *Albatross* was certainly a turning point. "I took ownership of my life and my decisions. Prior, things had been done for me or came easy. I never had to work for it. With the *Albatross* challenge, everything changed. It made a huge difference in me."

"Seems silly to pin it all on a job on a boat, but it tested your mettle; character. I went back to college a different person. I started getting As and found my place." She certainly did much better during her Sophomore year at Princeton.

When the next summer approached, her academic advisor strongly encouraged her to take a job more 'sciency' than working on a fishing boat. "I took a research job in Boston because I had to get serious about my life." But on weekends she'd often take a bus to the Cape and go out on the *Albatross* just as a volunteer, helping out and enjoying being back on the water. Dave let her ride along for free as she missed it greatly.

Cait went on to obtain her B.A in Molecular Biology from Princeton University and her M.D. from the Johnson Medical School at Rutgers University. She was an Assistant Professor of Medicine at the University of Pennsylvania and today is a practicing M.D. of internal medicine at Tulane University's Medical School. Filleting flounders aboard the *Albatross* in 2002 may have contributed to this successful career.

Amanda – Female Deck Hand during Captain Chip's Era

Turn the clock ahead twelve years from when Cait worked on the *Albatross*. It is now 2014. The Carrolls had taken ownership of the *Albatross* business nine years prior, Deck Hands were making very good wages and tips, and the whole working environment on the *Albatross* had transformed into a prosperous family business that embraced its Deck Hands and kept them around for years.

Amanda's story as a Deck Hand is much different than Cait's but equally gratifying and significant. Her spirit is best conveyed through her own words.

"Growing up, I watched the *Albatross* from my grandparents' deck on Harbor Road on Sesuit Neck as far back as I can remember. At that time, my siblings and I couldn't pronounce the boat's name, so we'd always say 'There goes the Alba-coss!' whenever we saw that big gray boat exit the jetty, cruise by on its way to Barnstable, or anchored by Tautog rock. That was back in the 1990s and into the 2000s.

The *Albatross* was always such a symbol and iconic part of Sesuit Harbor for the entirety of my memory, and I remember as a child saying it was one of my favorite boats in the harbor. Looking at it now,

I have no idea what I liked about it physically, but I remember as a kid how it looked so busy and bustling. Something that really peaked my curiosity and made me feel I wanted to be a part of it.

My brother Andrew started working as a Deck Hand on the *Albatross* years before me. One day I remember driving him down to Sesuit Harbor so he could meet with the Carrolls about a job as a Deck Hand. It wasn't long before he was employed full-time every summer, continuing to 2017.

When they employed Andrew as a Deck Hand, it was as if they accepted both of us as their second set of kids. When Andrew started working on the *Albatross*, I was working as a nanny. That June, the Carrolls recommended me for a job with Dennis Parasail & Jet Ski, which is owned and operated by a former Deck Hand of the *Albatross*. By the first week of July, I was working as greeter and jet ski instructor for that business."

Amanda was ecstatic because she had been trying to get a job in the harbor since she was thirteen. The Carrols had kindly recommended her to the parasailing company even before she had worked on the *Albatross* – a big break!

"They introduced me to connections within the harbor. A community I spent every summer living next to, but had yet to work within. I worked at the Marshside restaurant for years but it was the Carrolls who gave me the connection to get my foot in the door for marine work.

I worked the summers of 2012 and 2013 at Dennis Parasail with Captain Pete Gilrein who began his salty career as an *Albatross* Deck Hand. I remember spending all my free days either with my coworkers around the docks, with my brother Andrew or on the *Albatross* with the Carrolls. My foot in the door as a Deck Hand on the *Albatross* started during this time, while occasionally substituting for my Brother and working with another Deck Hand, Eddie. I would always try to help out to 'earn my spot' or 'earn my keep' whenever I went out on the boat. The Carrolls never charged me and only asked guests to tip the Deck Hands, so I used to do things like help to scrub the boat, etc.

After seeing the process so many times, filling in on the boat seemed relatively natural.

I also worked during the off-seasons for the Carrolls, helping to paint the *Albatross*, but it was not until the spring of 2014 that I was hired as a Deck Hand, at twenty-two years old. I had graduated from college that May, was saving up to pursue another degree and still trying to find a job. I started in the spring doing *Albatross* fishing trips and occasional educational trips with the Audubon Society as well. I was a full-time Deck Hand for the summer and into the fall.

That October, I started a career job using my degree within the field of Psychology but since I still had plans to attend graduate school, I worked whenever possible aboard the *Albatross* to save money. This continued through the summer of 2015. I could never get enough of it; it was always such a pleasure and a release to work on the water, be around the Carrolls and spend time with the other Deck Hands and my Brother that it never really felt like a job to me.

Summers within the harbor community were definitely the best times of my life. I met some of the most down-to-earth, hardworking people within that community; one I am still part of to this day. It opened up a lot of doors to numerous jobs, including the Lobster Roll dinner cruise boat as a waitress/bartender and the Sesuit Harbor Café."

Amanda's early life has certainly been intertwined with the *Albatross* and the Carroll family. She carries fond memories of her years as Deck Hand and recognizes the significance of being one of the few female Deck Hands.

"Most people were impressed that a girl was onboard and performing as a capable Deck Hand. One mom told me she was really happy her young daughter was seeing me work next to the boys as an equal. There was always the occasional customer that you felt had their doubts, but to those people, I just let my work and know-how speak for themselves."

I asked Amanda how she compared with the male Deck Hands. "I think we tended to be more diligent and patient with customers that were really struggling with their bait, reel or line. Not to say that the boys were not helpful, but sometimes on the water there is a 'do or die' sense where the fast learners catch the fish. I feel that girl Deck Hands paid fine attention to help the 'strugglers'.

I think families, especially those with young children, really enjoyed how we girls (Linnea, Sarah and I) interacted one-on-one with their kids. I have always loved kids and some of my favorite memories onboard were helping these 'little sponges for information' learn how to fish and love the water. It was always rewarding when you felt they really appreciated what they were soaking up."

On the topic of possible disadvantages for female Deck Hands, Amanda felt that "Naturally, guys are stronger. I had helped out on the boat for a couple seasons and understood the process and physical involvement. Being a college athlete, I liked to believe that I could handle both anchor weights, but when I was hired, I paid a little extra attention to my arms at the gym for the months leading up to the summer. I wanted to be able to perform every part of the job and I feared that if I couldn't pull the anchor I would not be taken seriously by the crew." She performed well, as expected, with her strong determination.

On a lighter side, she also remembers the fishing, occasional bad weather, pranks and funny stories. "Fishing was always best in the early summer and slower during the hottest months of July and August. When the water was warmest, it also meant a lot of dogfish, but that was pretty normal. I remember filleting around 60 fish apiece, each Deck Hand, so probably around 100 to 120 fish per trip. We always took a bet on who could guess the date of the first dogfish of the season."

She admitted that there was one (fairly minor) way she kept screwing up on the *Albatross*. "When working as Deck Hand for Captain Aidan Manning, we had a chum pot that we'd hang over the side of the boat to attract fish. It contained fish parts and clam guts in the perforated bucket so the juices would leach out. Well, I wasn't very good at holding onto the chum pot and I lost two of them. Shawney bought a third, beautiful replacement and I even lost the top of that one." It obviously wasn't important enough to justify firing this good worker.

"The repetition and skill of filleting fish after the trip was always so satisfying. I loved talking to the kids around the fish table, dissecting the guts of the fish to educate them and let them get their hands dirty. A kind of raw learning experience I feel lots of kids don't get to experience anymore."

And there were a few tasks the Deck Hands always hated. "North winds were a good time! Some nice four-foot rollers on a round-bottom boat made things interesting, but of course this was pretty nauseating to some tourists and that often meant bailing buckets to clean the head (toilet). Also cleaning the side of boat, if you catch my drift."

One of her amusing memories involved cleaning fish. "While filleting, a crowd of kids were on their tip-toes around the fish table. When I was a kid, I loved dissecting the fish carcasses with my Sister, right after my Dad had filleted them. We were not your typical girls growing up.

Whenever the opportunity arose aboard the *Albatross*, I loved teaching kids about basic fish anatomy while filleting. It was always funny to watch the looks on the mothers' faces as they watched their kids pick up fish stomachs, skin, eye balls, etc. One time I prepared and ate a bit of 'sushi' with some of the brave kids. It was the freshest fish, just brought on board and I convinced them they were in for quite the treat. I cleaned up the fish meat really nice and cut several small bites for the kids to try. As someone who's into raw tuna only, I pretended to like this raw morsel as if it were a delicacy. It was hilarious to watch most of the kids pretend the same thing even though some of their faces said quite the opposite. I then started laughing and said 'I actually think most raw fish is terrible.' and we had a bit of a laugh as the truth came out about what they actually thought!"

I asked Amanda if the Captains on the *Albatross* demonstrated a sense of humor. "Chip has always been a dictionary of jokes, all kinds of one-liners, so he always had an arsenal of jokes and puns, corny and hilarious alike. I don't know Dave Howes very well because he came aboard only a few times when I was working. As a female Deck Hand, I was looking for his seal of approval and I think I got the 'thumbs-up' by the end of one fishing trip, so that felt pretty good."

Reminiscing, Amanda has strong, positive feelings about her involvement with the *Albatross* and the entire Carroll family. "My *Albatross* years were swathed with invaluable lessons and memories of family, love, loyalty, work-ethic that came during a time of coming into adulthood and finding a way in our little corner of the world. The *Albatross* helped solidify these pillars and served as a foundation during a time of a lot of questions and sometimes fewer answers.

The Carrolls are some of the most generous and giving people I have ever met and throughout the years, they were there for me, even after college when I was between apartments on the Cape. They provided countless meals, many fishing trips, numerous job and school recommendations, life talks, advice, love and great company. The family-first atmosphere was something both my Brother and I could really relate to and appreciate. I became close with the entire family and spent a lot of time with Linnea and Sarah throughout the years."

Amanda and I spoke recently when she had her 'philosophical' mind in gear, thinking back about her *Albatross* days, albeit only a few years ago. To her, "Sesuit Harbor was kind of an energy 'hub' in my life, around which everything else is connected. Links to people, who became life-long friends, who also provided links to my many jobs in the harbor. These friends took me to geographies like Key West; they turned me on to Florida, where I later earned my B.S. in Nursing. All chain reactions that led to success and who I am."

Amanda also acknowledges that her time on the *Albatross* was excellent training for helping people of all ages, being safety minded, teaching children about fish anatomy and not being squeamish, and developing a positive, can-do attitude that prepared her for a medical career. Following her first year as Deck Hand on the *Albatross*, she obtained her B.S. in Psychology from Western New England University then her B.S. in Nursing from the University of Miami two years later. Since early 2017, she has been a Registered Nurse at the Cape Cod Hospital, specializing in Orthopedic and Neurologic care.

"If I'd had the experience I did within the harbor and on the *Albatross* earlier in my adolescence, I think I would have seriously considered pursuing a marine-related career."

No worries Amanda, you've done well.

14

Fishing Gear, Bait and Techniques

Fishing Gear

When the *Albatross* began operating in the mid-1960s, fishing gear was not very high-tech, especially that used for bottom fishing. Fisherman on boats used short rods and basic reels with cylindrical spools rather than 'spinning reels' that were new on the fishing tackle market. The long casting rods and 'fancy contraptions' (as the 'Old Timers' called the spinning reels) were used primarily for casting from the beach, so most people opted for 'boat rods' and conventional reels for bottom fishing.

During the first ten or so years, *Albatross* patrons were provided with a 'hand-line' free of charge. This conventional rig consisted of a natural-fiber line on a piece of thin wood that was H-shaped. The line was wrapped around the horizontal part of the H to prevent tangling. But of course during fishing, the novice would dump the slack line on the deck and it would immediately become tangled with itself and anything nearby. The Deck Hand would always come to the rescue.

What's most memorable about the old hand-lines is they were coated with tar to prevent rotting of the natural-fiber line. During the line manufacturing process, the tar was heated and allowed to penetrate the fibers of the line. When the fishermen were given new lines at the beginning of the season, they looked strong and dark from the tar coating and had an oily smell. With the heat of day, their hands would become a black mess from the tar. Only strong detergent would rid their hands of the tar at the end of the trip. To this day, whenever I smell tar I immediately remember the hand-lines on the early days of the *Albatross*.

For the exorbitant fee of 50¢ for the four-hour trip, Captain Dave would rent a rod-and-reel rig to the avid fishermen who were convinced they would land more fish than if they used the meager hand-line. This was disproven hundreds of times over the years.

When novices would use a rod and reel for the first time, the Deck Hands always cringed. Often, the fishermen would forget to put their thumb on the spool of line when lowering the sinker. A large 'bird's nest' would immediately develop in the reel when slack line occurred – another task for the Deck Hand.

Worse yet, the novices would attempt to cast their hook and sinker to a spot some distance from the boat (where the fishing might be better?). This not only increased the chance for a bird's nest, but would create peril for neighboring fishermen. More frequently than the Captain would like, there'd be a scream on deck, signaling that someone had been hooked by a casting novice. Very rarely would they be significant injuries that required the vessel to return to shore for medical assistance for the hooked person.

'Super Sport' fishermen would often bring two or three expensive rod and reel rigs aboard, thinking they would out-fish everyone else. They used complex rigs with two-hook spreaders or three hooks in the vertical but these rarely out-fished the simple one-hook rig with a single sinker attached. To this day, the *Albatross* provides only a single small hook that is ideal for the very small mouth of winter flounder. When larger hooks are used to lure larger prey, they totally prevent hooking of winter flounder.

Hand-lines have been phased out for decades on the *Albatross*; a rod and reel is provided to all patrons within the price of the four-hour trip.

Bait

Clams

In the early days of *Albatross* fishing, quahogs were the primary bait. Dave purchased large burlap bags of live quahogs from the Cultured Clam Corporation, located at the end of Chapin Beach near the Bass Hole. He would keep the submerged bags in a 'car' – a large box made with wooden slats to allow harbor water to flow through, as the car was locked adjacent to the dock. The Deck Hand would remove a couple bucketsful of whole quahogs for each trip. The quahogs would last many weeks while submerged but the average-size clam would only yield a half dozen baits.

Quahog shells are strong and very hard to open so Dave built a bait-cutting board that had a strong, steel dome at its center, ideal for smashing the shells. By hand, the Deck Hands would smash the shells on the metal piece rather than open them with a knife, which was much slower. Shell shrapnel was common for everyone situated close to the bait board; clam juice as well.

A substitute bait for quahogs was local sea clams (surf clams as they're called south of Massachusetts). In the early years of *Albatross* fishing, Dave's father Skip would frequently take his wooden, 1897-vintage, motorized Crosby Cat boat into the Bay to drag for sea clams, a plentiful species in sand bottom east of Sesuit Harbor. They were large and made excellent bait for flounder fishing. Each sea clam would yield about twenty good baits.

Skip could normally drag up a couple bushels (one bushel equals nine gallons) in an hour or two, then he'd pull alongside the *Albatross* to provide Dave with bait.

This bait service was quite routine but Dave and Skip had a sense of humor so they decided to play-act a bit, making a skit of Sea Captains meeting at sea. It went like this: Dave would see the Cat boat passing by and would wave for it to come closer. When nearby, Dave would holler "Hey Cap, been dragging for clams?"

"Yup" Skip would say; nothing more.

"Get any?"

"Yup"

"Can I buy a bushel for bait?"

"Yup"

The deal was done, Dave would pass Skip a $20 bill so everyone could see that he had to pay dearly for the fresh bait, for which Dave didn't charge his customers. His Father would give him the bill back, that evening ashore. Dave probably paid for Skip's fuel but the comic relief was the best part for the actors involved.

'Woims'

There were other Super Sports who insisted that sea worms were more effective for floundering than quahogs or sea clams. Some of the most adamant personalities were from New York; experienced flounder men who had fished Sheepshead Bay for years. With their New York accent they'd called them 'woims' and boasted about all their tricks for floundering.

Initially, Dave held his ground. "Clams are the only thing on the menu and they work fine every time." Even if worms were better, Dave wasn't about to change his way of business because worms were expensive and much more work to keep alive than clams. And back in the early days, it was easy to catch fish no matter what you used for bait. Later, Dave offered worms for sale as an alternative bait and found they worked quite well.

Captain Chip continues to sell worms so fishermen can have their choice of bait. It's still uncertain which bait fishes best for winter flounder but opinions are strong among the avid fishermen. Some even say that pieces of squid fish best. And bare, shiny hooks work best for mackerel!

Bait balls

No matter how many times Dave said that it's best to use only a small piece of clam on the hook for floundering, the Super Sports would often load up their hooks with a big wad of clam meat. No way could that fit into the small mouth of a winter flounder. It could be munched on for many minutes before the fish's mouth felt the metal hook. And the adept bait-stealers could chew at-will without risk of being hooked.

But the biggest problem with the bait-ball approach to fishing was the inevitable attraction of the dreaded dogfish. Dangle the wad of clams in the bottom current and a school of dogs would quickly get the scent and appear in minutes, with no chance they'd head away. All the lines would be snagged together within a big tangle beneath the boat, even with only a few fish hooked. Thirty minutes of unsnarling would be necessary, then the boat would have to move to another fishing spot. The Deck Hands hated seeing bait balls going over the side.

Fishing Techniques

It's important to first acknowledge that the majority of the patrons that go on the *Albatross* are first-timers. Not just on this boat trip, but first-timers at fishing in the 'ocean', if that's how they wished to characterize Cape Cod Bay. The frequent question of "What do I do if I catch a whale?" is a clear indication of their fishing prowess.

Over the first forty years of *Albatross* trips, Dave had perfected the training program for flounder fishing, with great brevity. "Lower it to the bottom, reel it up a foot and keep it there. Every thirty seconds give it a quick tug and see if you've got a fish on." That was it – thirty words. 'Sounds simple but not when you realize that most of the 'fishermen' didn't even know how to lower the rig nor feel when the sinker had hit bottom. Most couldn't visualize whether the bottom was ten feet down or abyssal depth. Dave's detailed fishing instructions were forgotten within minutes and each person would develop their own special technique.

Some novices would look around to see what the Super Sports were doing. Other techniques developed, including 'sinker bouncing': a common technique with constant up and down motion. Some thought fish would be attracted by the sound of the weight hitting bottom.

The fidgety technique was used by others, with constant jiggling of the bait. The 'RIP' technique also was popular, requiring no effort at all. The sinker was initially dropped to the bottom and thereafter forgotten. The fisherman was free to have a beer, talk with buddies, visit the bathroom or nap. After a while (e.g., ten minutes or until the Captain said to haul-in because the boat was going to move to another spot) the 'fisherman' would reel in the line. Frequently, there was no bait left on the hook but on rare occasion there was a fish on the line who had grown accustomed to having a hook in his mouth; no fighting ensued. The Deck Hand would just net the near-dead specimen.

Some Super Sports insisted on occupying their ‘favorite spot’ on the stern rail but other patrons were more concerned about where they’d get the most tanning during the trip. The aft rail was actually a good spot because when the boat is anchored, chum and lost bait from other lines might drift aft and possibly attract more fish near the stern than near the bow of the boat. However, the wind often pushes the boat crosswise from the direction of the tidal flow so that technique is void much of the time.

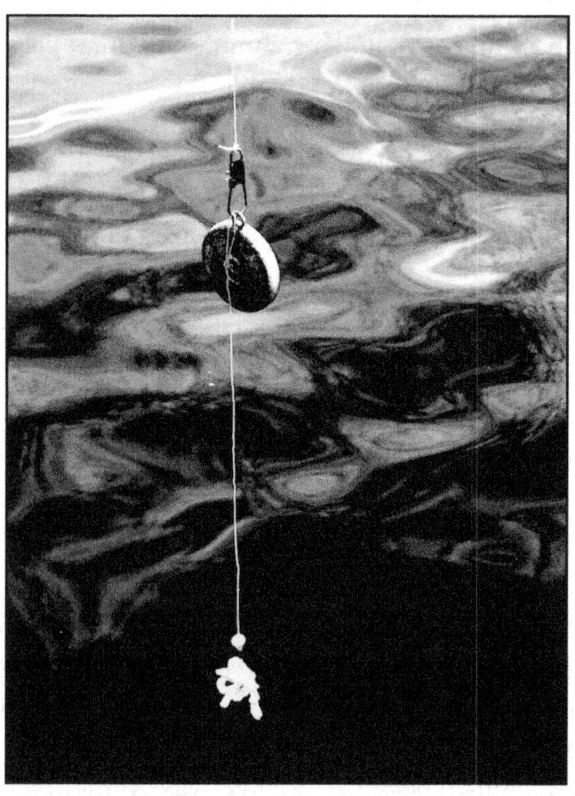

15

Fishing Spots

Defying its title, this chapter does NOT provide the location of the *Albatross*' favorite fishing locations. But it does share the history and methodology of positioning for these coveted fishing 'hotspots' or 'honey holes' as the Old Timers called them. And to this day, Captain Dave will not share his positions with anyone, not even me! I suppose Captain Chip now has them under lock and key.

Back in 1965, the first *Albatross* was equipped with a depth 'flasher' (fathometer), compass and a local chart for navigation. On foggy days, Dave paid "damn close attention" to his course, speed and duration of steaming to determine the position of the vessel, especially when returning to Sesuit Harbor. This technique is called Dead Reckoning (DR) by sailors, originating from Elizabethan times (1605-1615). DR is a method of estimating the position of a vessel without using astronomical observations (i.e., sextant, sun azimuth, stars, etc.) or electronic means. It predicts a new position based upon an original position and the subsequent course and distance traveled. Some say DR is short for Deduced Reckoning, based upon where you've been.

With the advancement of micro-electronics in the late 1970s, LORAN-C radio navigation systems became the primary marine navigation network in coastal seas. While it offered relatively good position resolution, its accuracy was no better than hundreds of feet. Thus, it was not useful for the *Albatross*' navigation near shore and in proximity to submerged objects.

For repositioning the *Albatross* on the coveted fishing hotspots, Dave had to resort to the low-tech, tried-and-true navigation method called 'Pine Tree Navigation'. No electricity, no electronics, no calculators, no charts nor rulers, just a compass and a hand-written notebook. Maybe a pair of binoculars. This method always was and still is, based upon visual triangulation with distinct objects on shore.

Fifty years ago, Scargo Tower was easily seen from offshore as it stood well above the tree line a half-mile south of Dennis village. A few large town-owned water towers, radio antennae and 'fire towers' (tall observation towers manned during the fire season) also stood proudly above the vegetation, miles back from the shoreline. The bayside dunes had only a sprinkling of small summer cottages; not like today.

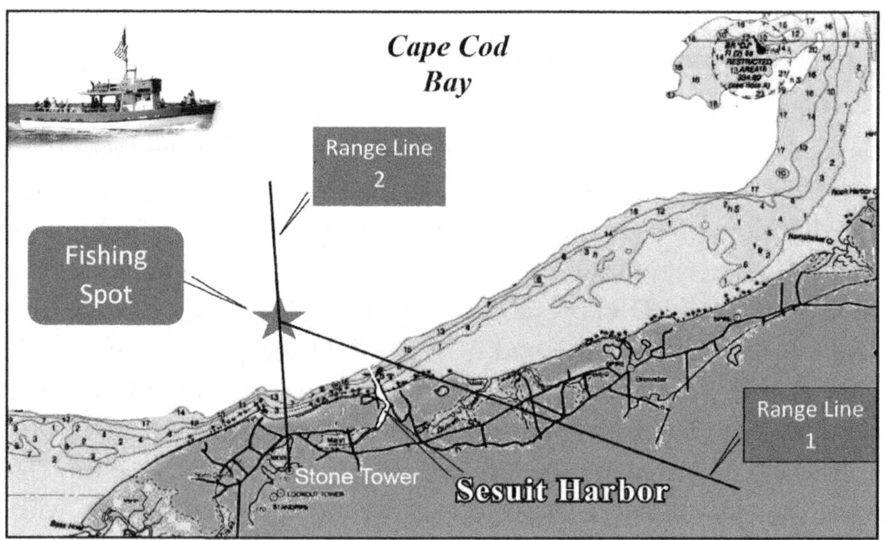

Determining ranges for a good fishing spot.

The Old Timers had a negative attitude about living near the beach in those days: "No one in their right mind would want to live year-round on the bluffs as the winter winds from the north would howl through the drafty, single-pane window frames. 'Couldn't keep your damn oil lamp from blowing out.' That attitude changed in the 1980s when certain people had enough money to build well-insulated homes, some folks occupying them year-round; imagine that!

In the 1960s, Dave knew who owned each of the houses along the shore from Quivet Creek to the Bass Hole at the Dennis-Yarmouth line. It was easy to notice when the Brewster fire tower was lined up exactly with Bill Stone's mansion on the hill just west of Sesuit. And if Scargo Tower was positioned above Luby's house, it made for a good 'range' as the two 'range lines' or 'cuts' were separated by a significant angle (preferably, sixty-degrees or more). The boat was located exactly where the range lines met, offshore.

If a good 'mess' of fish was caught while anchored at that spot, Dave would sketch the houses, towers and the two range lines in the notebook and name it something, often unrelated. For example, maybe his dog brought home a skunk last night, so that range got named 'Skunk'.

Over the forty years Dave ran the *Albatross*, he located many good honey holes which became ranges with funny names (e.g., Fatman, ZZ-Top, etc.) This navigation technique was considerably more accurate than using LORAN-C, especially if the boat was carefully anchored with recognition of wind 'set' and the direction of the tidal current at that particular time.

Like all systems that degrade or become obsolete, so did the Pine Tree Navigation network offshore Dennis. What happened was that the fire towers were gradually disassembled, the trees grew up higher than Scargo Tower and some of the water towers were replaced. Worse yet, most of the original cottages on the bluffs were torn down, some being replaced by 'New York mansions' with unknown ownership, at least from Dave's standpoint.

Note: Many Dennis Elders consistently had poor attitudes toward New Yorkers and the damn Yankees. (Likely because the New Yorkers who visited Dennis had considerably more money than the Dennis locals.) Consequently, if someone had enough money to build a large house on the bluff in Dennis, "...they must be New Yorkers!"

It was fortunate that accurate GPS navigation came along in the late 1990s so the *Albatross* Captains could determine accurate positions for each of the cherished ranges. I'll be 'damned if I know' whether Dave actually used GPS. Maybe Captain Chip uses high-tech navigation to position his boat on the best ranges today. I suspect he has all the *Albatross* honey holes entered as GPS waypoints.

Note: My Father grew up in Dennis village and had some amusing expressions that perpetuated the local, antiquated slang. For example, if he had more clams in his bucket than his friend, he'd say "I've got a damn sight more than you! You've only got foyve." (five, pronounced in Cape Cod tongue).

For some reason, he was not keen on putting a name on his boat that was berthed in a town slip. Over the years, he got damn sight tired of everyone asking him "What's the name of your boat?"

He'd always reply, "Damned if I know!"

As the years went on, he became even less patient, mumbling the same answer, which sounded like a single word, "Dam'f'I-know".

Fed up with the boat naming matter, the next year he painted one word on the transom: "DAMFINO"

16

Fish Species Caught

The purpose of this chapter is to illustrate the wide variety of fish caught aboard the *Albatross* over the 50-plus years of fishing in Cape Cod Bay. The species are placed in groups of desirability for consumption (according to the author's biased Cape Cod palate) and relative frequency of catch. Remember, there is no guarantee that a fisherman will catch a given species on a single fishing trip, or anything for that matter. Fish populations and fishermen's abilities are beyond the control of the *Albatross* Captain and Deck Hands.

Note: Where sizes of fish are mentioned below, these are typical lengths caught aboard the *Albatross*; larger fish may be caught elsewhere in deeper Massachusetts waters. Furthermore, sizes given do not represent the legal size for the species, as these may change annually based upon Massachusetts fisheries regulations. Fish below legal size are always released by *Albatross* crew.

Commonly Caught Species – Prime Eating

Flounder Type	Jaw size	Thickness	Gill position (top view)
Winter flounder	Small	Normal	Right
Fluke	Large	Thinner	Left
Four spot flounder	Large	Very thin	Left
Windowpane flounder	Large	Thinnest	Left

Winter Flounder ***(probably 80-90% of the catch on a given day)***

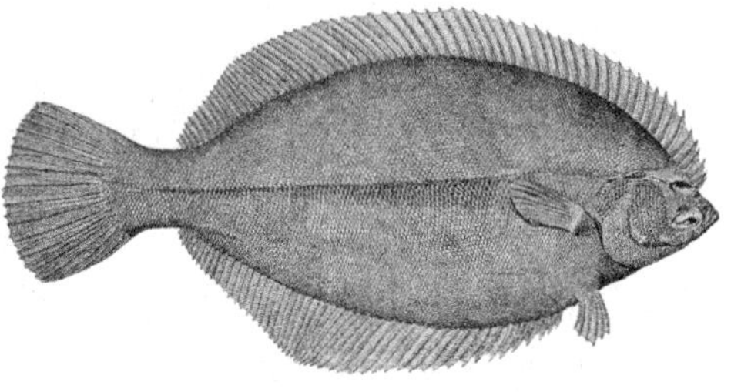

- The prime target, caught throughout the summer.
- Other names: blackback, lemon sole, flatfish
- Very small mouth with no teeth.
- Gills are located on right side of head looking downward.

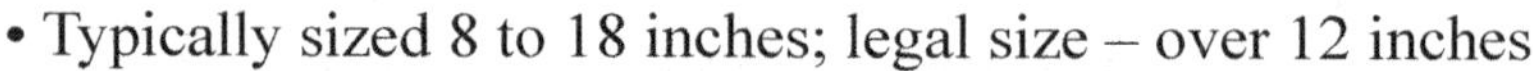

- Typically sized 8 to 18 inches; legal size – over 12 inches
- Excellent eating and a moderate fight for a light fish.

Fluke

- Other names: summer flounder, flatfish, doormat, flattie, sole, plaice
- Large mouth with significant teeth.
- Gills are located on left side of head looking downward.
- Good eating but thinner fillets than winter flounder.
- Excellent fight for a light fish.
- Typically sized 12 to 22 inches.

Four Spot Flounder

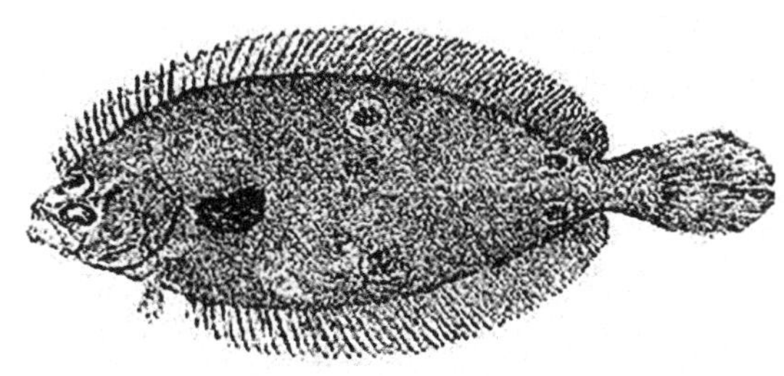

- Other names: four-eyed flounder, foureyed sole, four spotted fluke
- Nearly identical to fluke except for the four spots on top side.
- Fillets are generally too thin for filleting.
- Much smaller than fluke, less than 12 inches.

Windowpane Flounder

- Other names: sand dab, sundial, spotted flounder, sand flounder, Papermouth
- Cousin to the fluke but extremely thin with ribs bones visible through transparent skin.
- Insufficient fillet thickness regardless of fish length.
- Typically less than 12 inches.

Black Sea Bass

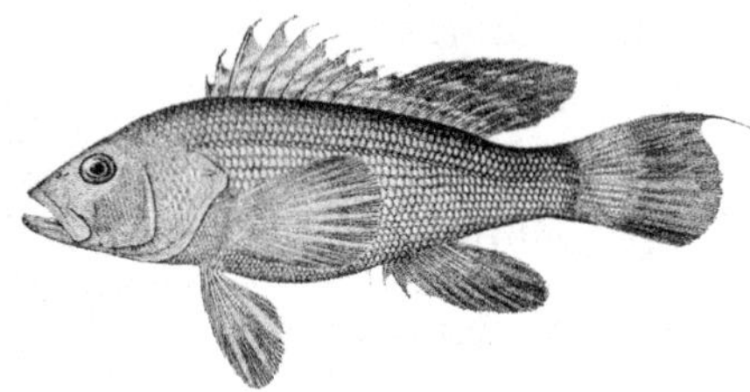

- Other names: seabass, humpback, rock bass, black will, squirrel bass, Hunan
- An ideal catch, either during late spring or early fall.
- Typically sized 12 to 20 inches; excellent eating.

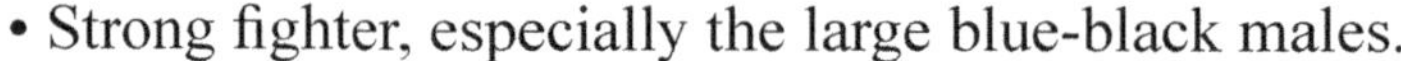

- Strong fighter, especially the large blue-black males.

Tautog

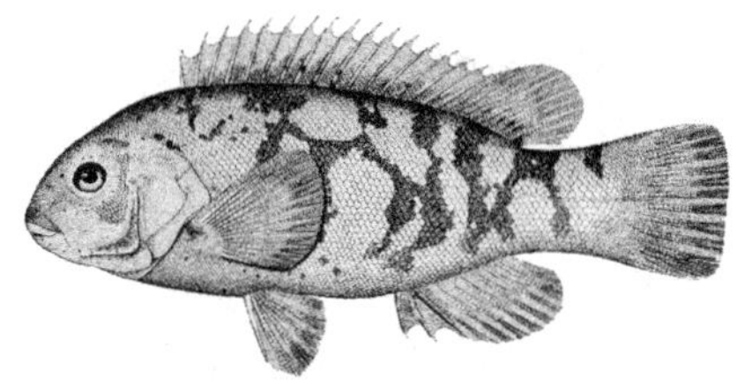

- Originally named by the Narragansett Indians of Rhode Island.
- Other names: black fish, tog, white chin, oyster fish, black porgy
- An excellent fighter with strong flavor – good for chowder.
- Typically sized 12 to 20 inches; heavy for their length.

Red Hake

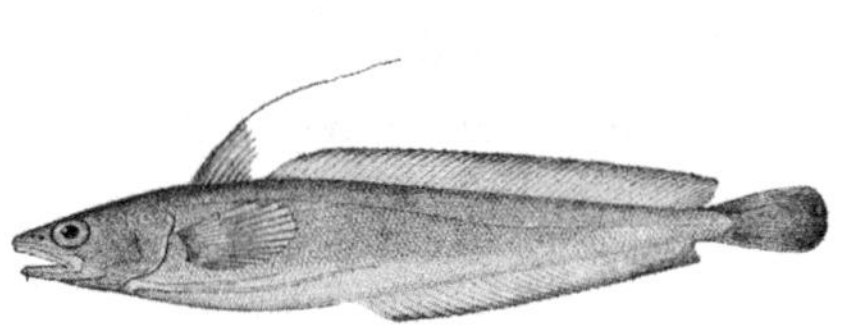

- Other names: squirrel hake, ling, mud hake
- Moderate fighter with good flavor from soft meat.
- Within the family of cod and haddock, originally from Ireland.
- Has a small barbel extending beneath the lower jaw, typical of cod family.
- Typically sized 10 to 18 inches.

Mackerel

- Excellent fighter and fast swimmer, normally caught at mid-depth or surface.
- Red, bloody meat as they're in the tuna family.
- Typically sized 8 to 12 inches.

Nuisance Catch

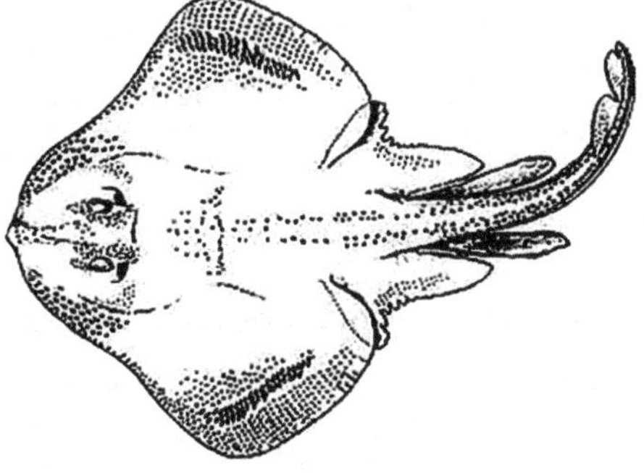

Skate

- Incorrect names: ray or stingray (different from skates)
- A trash fish to most anglers.
- Some people eat the white meat from the cartilaginous wings.
- Circular pieces cut from wings are sometimes sold as fake scallops.
- Typically sized 12 to 18 inches but can be much larger.

Cunner

- Other names: bergall, perch, chogset, choggie,
- Similar to, but much smaller than tautog, with orange/brown coloring.
- The smallest and most adept 'bait stealer', with teeth protruding forward.

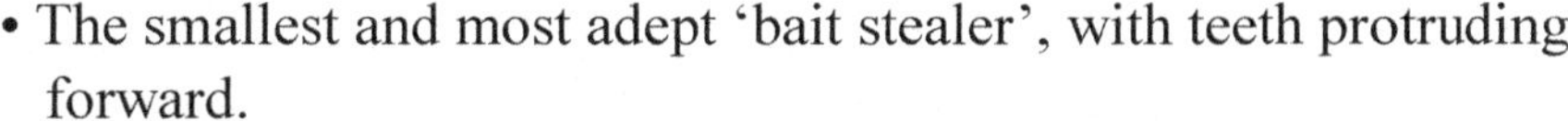

- Too small and bony to eat.
- Typically sized 6 to 10 inches.

Spiny Dogfish

- Other names: spurdog, cape shark
- Incorrect name: sand shark (a different, larger shark)
- A small, slender, small-toothed shark with spikes ahead of two dorsal fins.
- A popular food source in Canada, Europe and Great Britain but not in the U.S.
- Spawns babies during summer months, with many released during landing aboard.
- Typically sized 24 to 36 inches.

Sea Robin

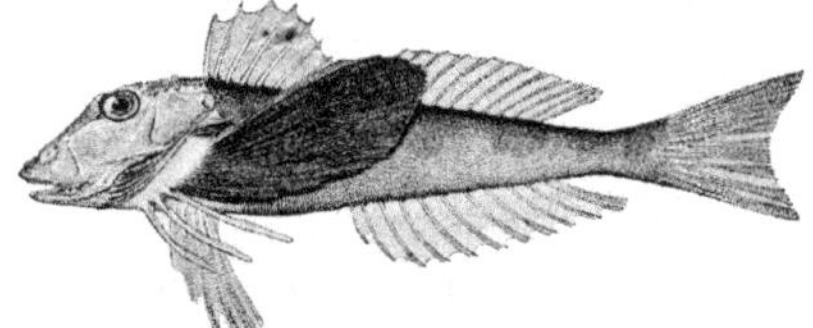

- Other names: croaker, gurnard (from the sound it makes)
- Incorrect name: sculpin – a different fish
- The robin name originates from its orange color and its side fins that resemble wings.
- They have three small feet on each side beneath.
- Recently, people have begun eating their meat but without widespread acceptance.
- Typically sized 6 to 10 inches.

Tomcod

- Other names: tommy cod, frostfish
- Similar in appearance to the larger cod.
- Sized less than 8 inches.

Electric Ray

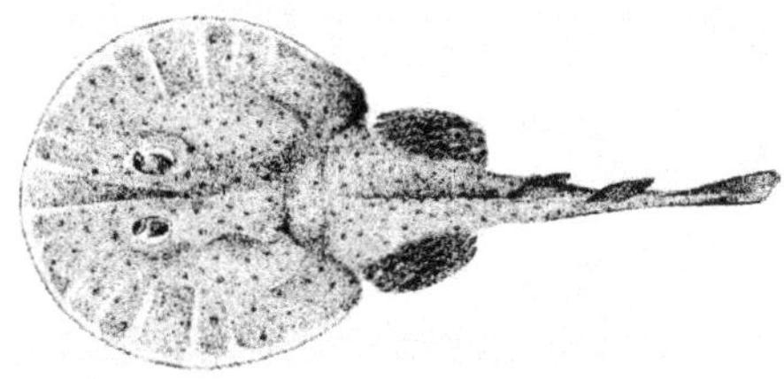

- Near-circular shape is distinctly different from skates which have pointed snouts and wings.
- Sized about 15 to 30 inches across.

Seldom Caught but Desirable

Cod

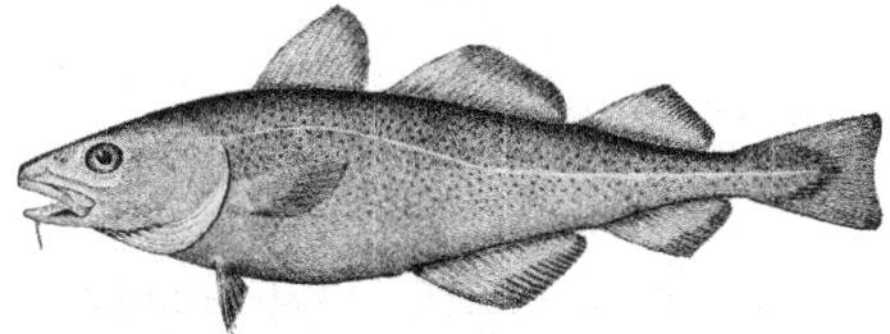

- Other names: scrod (small cod), codfish, codling,
- Incorrect name: tommy cod (a different, smaller fish)
- Ideal catch with a strong fight and good meat; meat may contain worms during summer.
- Brown with spots on both sides.
- Has an extended barbel beneath the lower jaw.
- Excellent eating.
- Typically sized 12 to 24 inches in Cape Cod Bay;

Monkfish

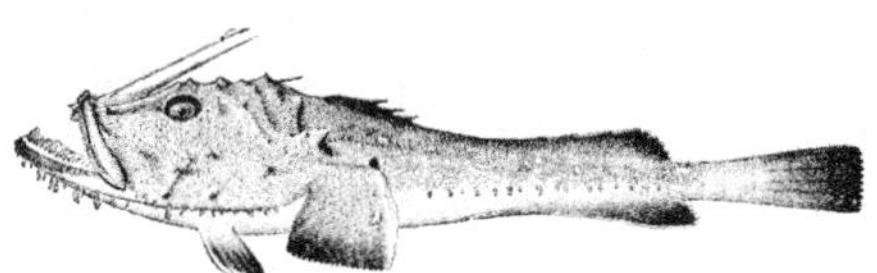

- Other names: goosefish, angler fish
- Prehistoric looking fish with very large horizontal mouth Good fighter.
- Excellent eating from flesh on large tail sections.
- Sometimes wash ashore dead from having attempted to swallow sea birds whole.
- Typically sized 20 to 30 inches.

Bluefish

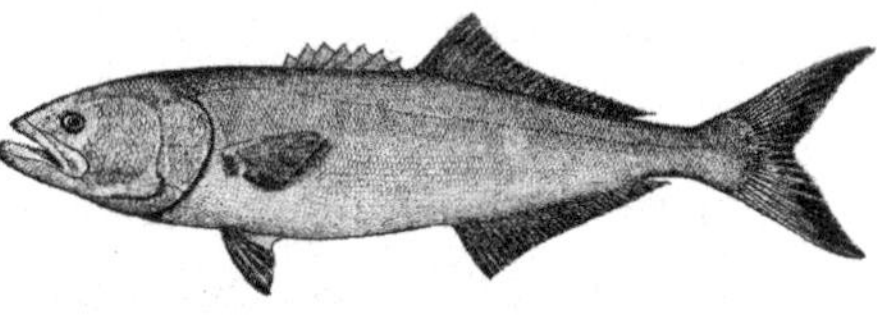

- Other names: snappers, tailor, cocktail blues, choppers, gators, slammers
- Strong, fast pelagic fish that give an excellent fight.
- Dangerous teeth.
- Dark, bloody meat but good eating if baked with drainage.
- Typically sized 15 to 24 inches.

American Eel

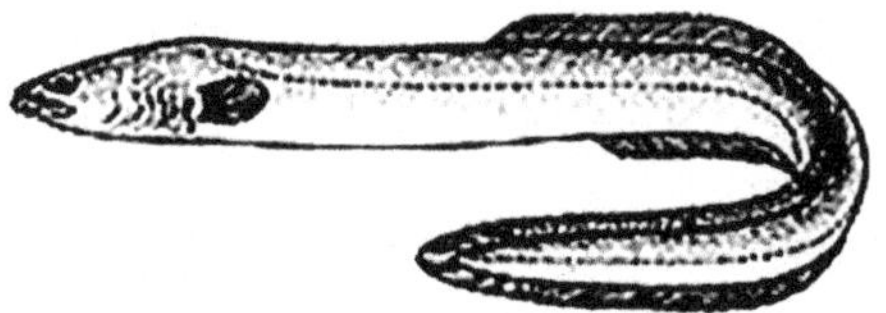

- Other names: common eel, freshwater eel, Atlantic eel
- Typically sized 15 to 30 inches.

Ocean Pout

- Other names: American eel pout, mutton fish
- Incorrect name: conger eel (a different fish)
- The head is large and wider than the elongated body.
- No barbel as it is not in the cod family.
- The mouth has numerous medium size molar-like teeth and fleshy lips.
- Typically sized 15 to 26 inches.

Cusk Eel

- Other names: tusk, torsk, lumb
- Another cousin to the cod, with the same brown coloring and barbel on the chin.
- Fins of the cod are replaced with a single fin from front to back as with eels.
- Elongated, heavy bodied fish, absent of scales, with a flattened head. The mouth is large with numerous medium-sized sharp teeth. Typically caught in water deeper than
- Cape Cod Bay. Good eating
- Typically sized 12 to 20 inches

Pollock

- Other names: green cod, coalfish, Boston bluefish,
- Similar to the haddock, but with green sides and a white line along each side.
- Strong fighter often at mid-depth like mackerel.
- Good eating; typically sized 12 to 20 inches.

Striped Bass

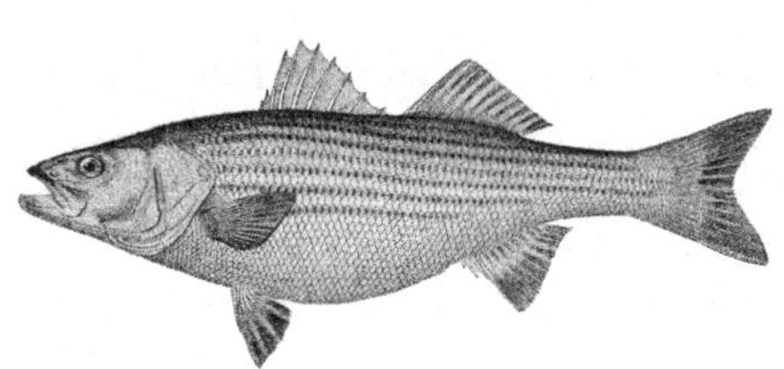

- Other names: striper, schoolie, rockfish, linesider, squidhound, cow
- A very rare catch from the Albatross.
- Most people believe they are good eating.
- None have been caught on the Albatross above the minimum length limit (28 inches).
- Typically sized 18 to 40 inches.

Whiting

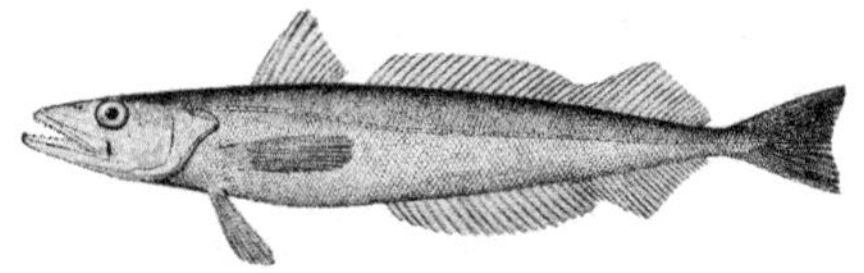

- Other names: silver hake, New England hake
- There is no danger of confusing it with red hake as it lacks chin barbels and its ventrals are ordinary finlike whereas those of hakes are long feelers.
- Typically sized 8 to 14 inches.

Haddock

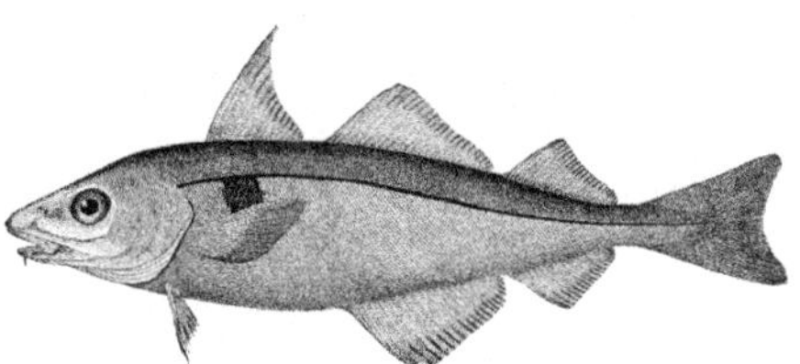

- Other names: silver cod, scrod (small haddock), finnan haddie
- A cousin to the cod, with silver color and a black line along each side.
- Excellent eating, typically sized 12 to 18 inches.

Lobster

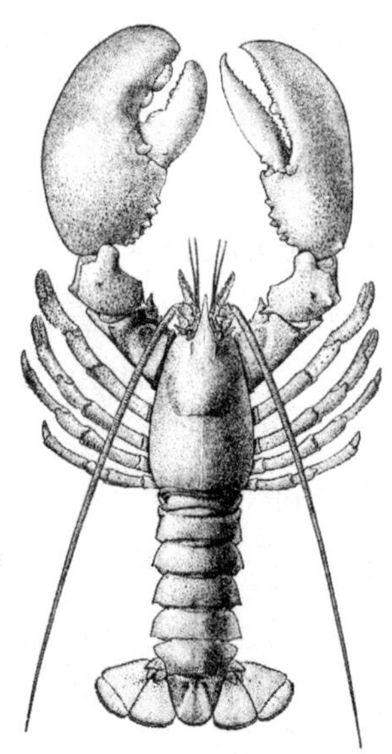

- A few have been caught with fishing line.
- Largest was 12 pounds.
- Prohibited from landing unless the fisherman has a lobster license.
- Egg-bearing females must be set free.

Observed Only

Whales

Leatherback Turtles

Dolphin Mammals

Ocean Sunfish

Blue Sharks

Giant Bluefin Tuna

Basking Sharks

Atlantic Killer Whales, offshore Barnstable in the mid-1970s, a pod of five.

17

Amusing Stories from Deck Hands and Captains

This section presents many amusing stories from the *Albatross* Captains and numerous Deck Hands (purposely kept anonymous). The stories were provided to me in writing or via conversation.

Although I have not included quotation marks, much of the text represents their first-person contributions, with only minor editing. The order of stories is not based upon significance nor level of humor; rather, they are intentionally presented in random order.

Little girl catches the most fish

A family came out fishing one day and they brought their young daughter who had long braided hair. She was so small she could barely see over the rail of the boat. She was using a hand-line to fish and kept pulling in fish one after the other; maybe six to eight fish before the trip was half over.

There was a man fishing next to her who Captain Dave categorized as a 'Hero'. The gung-ho fisherman had brought many rods, a big tackle box and had sporting patches sewn all over his fishing shirt. But he couldn't catch a fish! As the hours passed, his frustration level kept rising, especially as he heard the little girl again say "I caught another fish, Daddy."

Hake butter

Captain George on the *Osprey* encountered his share of amusing tourists as well. One day, a fashionable passenger wearing white shorts and a white tennis sweater had been complaining all afternoon about not catching enough fish. After a few hours of this, George was quite frustrated and wanted to tell the guy to walk the plank. Eventually, the guy caught a large hake. Anyone who knows hake is fully aware that they have a large stomach that is very soft and quick to release substantial volumes of offensive brown juice from the non-sunshine side of its anatomy. Without the man realizing what was happening, George skillfully aimed the fish's lower orifice toward the passenger and gave the fish a good strong squeeze. Masterfully, he succeeded in painting the man's sweater a horrific and scented brown. Of course he apologized, but nearly bit his tongue off trying to hold back his laughter.

Tossing their catch overboard – by accident

Here's a prank that was not intentional, but the end result was perfect. There was a father and son who were on an afternoon fishing trip. They caught about ten fish between the two of them but both had bad attitudes. At the end of the trip, the father was very paranoid that the bucket containing his fish fillets would be accidentally dumped overboard. I assured him that I had never lost any fish, whole or in pieces.

When I wasn't paying attention, the other Deck Hand went to rinse out the fillet buckets and unintentionally dumped this guy's fish overboard, right in front of him. I felt like such an idiot, I didn't know what to say to him.

Saving only the big flounders

There was a very nice man from Long Island, NY, who came fishing on the *Albatross* multiple times each summer. He was the first to board the boat when he came fishing and would grab his favorite spot at the port-side stern. He always carried his two rods, tackle box and fished with dual-hook spreaders on each rod. A 'meat fisherman' or 'Super Sport' we'd say.

His goal was to bring as many flounder home as possible and he started keeping undersized flounder, which pissed me off. Dave always suggested that any flounder smaller than twelve inches in length be released. Regardless, the fisherman would keep even the undersized fish because where he normally fished, only very small flounder were caught. Of course, he was occasionally excited to catch the large fish of Cape Cod Bay.

I would often grab a rod and start fishing while cutting bait at the rear of the boat, next to this fisherman. One time I hooked a very large flounder, reeled it in and landed it with a net. I took it off the hook, looked at it briefly and threw it overboard right next to the fisherman.

"What are you doing?" the fisherman asked in disbelief.

"Too small – we don't keep those." The fisherman was shocked by my action but I think he got the message. Every so often, I would have to remind him again by throwing another large fish back in the water. I had to teach this lesson to other people as well, a few times.

Overall, this fisherman became a great customer, returning year after year with a good attitude. One time he brought a newspaper clipping from New York to show Dave. It was a rave review he had written about the *Albatross* and the big flounders that could be caught in Cape Cod Bay.

A final anecdote: I (author) became friends with this fisherman as I was working as Deck Hand. Once I invited him to go flounder fishing in my own small boat from Sesuit Harbor. The short story is that we caught a galvanized washtub of flounders in an afternoon. When Dave heard that I had taken one of his customers out for a free trip, he was so angry I thought I was going to get fired, at fifteen.

Fisherman who was never happy

One day a man and his son came out fishing and it proceeded to be the best fishing trip we ever had. When we returned to shore, they had a bag so full of fish they had to drag it up the dock to their car. They came back to fish nearly every day that week but all they did was bitch because they weren't catching as many as the first trip. They happened to hit the best fishing trip in forty years but they weren't happy because it didn't repeat each day thereafter.

When a lobster isn't a lobster

On one fishing trip we had a family from the Midwest who were totally enamored with lobsters. They said it was the one special treat in their house and that even their two kids, aged nine and eleven, requested lobster as their special birthday dinner. Apparently, anytime this family dined out, it was for lobster.

They weren't very knowledgeable about where lobsters come from. They knew they were caught in the Northeast and that they were only available in Kansas in the restaurants.

When we got to the fishing ground, we were surrounded by a bunch of lobster traps. Not knowing what the surface floats were for, they were very excited to hear they were attached to lobster traps. Over the next two hours of bottom fishing, I and the Deck Hands were bombarded with questions about how do you catch the lobsters, what do you use for bait, how many to a trap, what is a trawl and every other question you can think about lobster fishing.

On the way in, they came up to the wheelhouse with even more questions. I said we could pull up one of my traps, as long as no one objected to arriving in the harbor ten minutes late. A quick poll said no one was in a hurry, so on the return we stopped to pull one of my traps near Tautog Rock.

Wanting to put on a good show, I was delighted when the Deck Hand pulled a trap over the rail that had two nice lobsters inside. I was confused with the family's lack of enthusiasm when we pulled two beautiful, large lobsters out of the trap.

The Mother immediately said "That's not a lobster."

I said, "Yes, it is. This one's a male and this one is a female, and they are both of legal size."

But she still protested, saying "But they are not red!"

Size matters, for fish too

One day a fisherman started screaming, "Net, net, net!" Everyone knew that a big fish was coming to the surface and a net was needed to land the great catch. Captain Chip happened to be the first crewmember to arrive with a net and he quickly snatched the fish from the water. To everyone's surprise, the fish was very small.

Embarrassed, the fisherman admitted "It looked so much bigger underwater."

Chip replied, tongue in cheek. "That's why you never stand up in a Jacuzzi."

Across the boat, there was a very old lady fishing; she must have been in her nineties. When she heard the comment about the Jacuzzi, she broke out laughing so hard that Chip thought she was going to fall over the side of the boat. Very funny.

Thereafter, Deck Hands would joke about two size categories of fish: A Keeper or an Out-of-Water Keeper.

Albatross Money – A Mother's Term

Over the first few decades of *Albatross* operations, the majority of Deck Hands were young and lived at home with their parents. Typically, the mother would deliver sandwiches at lunchtime and wash their fish-scented laundry after the Deck Hand returned from the two fishing trips each day. Some mothers kept a bucket of Lysol at the back door to receive the smelly clothes before the Deck Hand was allowed to enter the house.

As fish filleting became a lucrative, ancillary income for the Deck Hands, they would bring home many dollar bills stuffed in their pockets. Sometimes the boys would forget about the money, leaving it in pockets after undressing. Unaware, the mother would run the '*Albatross* money' through the cycle of the automatic washer.

A worse scenario was when the Deck Hand removed the smelly '*Albatross* money' from their pockets and stuffed it into their dresser drawer adjacent to other clothes. After a week, the money would really wreak, to the mother's frustration. When *Albatross* mothers get together, this is a common topic of discussion.

Albatross filleters: maybe the world's fastest?

An *Albatross* Deck Hand later became a medic in the Army stationed in South Korea. He enjoyed cooking and one day wanted to make dinner for all of his friends. At a local fish market, he selected eight fish for a meal that evening, then told the Korean store owner "We'll have a competition to see who can fillet fish fastest. I'll fillet four and you fillet four. If I fillet my four fish quicker than you, all eight fish are free for me. If you finish first then I will pay you twice the price for the fish."

The store owner was probably thinking "Stupid American, this is my job."

Proudly demonstrating his *Albatross* filleting skills, the Deck Hand filleted his four fish before the store owner had started on his third fish. The Deck Hand clearly won the competition and got the eight fish for free, plus bragging rights forever aboard the *Albatross*.

Catching a Stripper – not a Striper

A few years ago, a group of passengers were having their bachelor party aboard the boat. It was a group of seven and all were seated along the port rail. They were a nice group enjoying the fishing.

About mid-way thru the trip, one of them hooked something big. It was pulling out line as fast as he could pull it in and all of his friends, as well as half the people on the port rail, retrieved their lines to give him best access. He fought this thing for a good five minutes before one of the Deck Hands realized the busy fisherman was hooked up with a young passenger on the starboard rail.

A Deck Hand first retrieved the line from the young passenger, with the other line still tangled with it. Next, the Deck Hand started messing with the line of the fisherman from the port side. They pulled on the line fast to simulate a real fish that was sounding, then let it go slack like the prey was charging toward the boat. Apparently, the fisherman had forgotten we were fishing for flounder, not marlin.

After about ten minutes of this playing and while the fisherman was oblivious to the laughter on the starboard side of the boat, the Deck Hand put a dollar bill on the fisherman's hook and released it into the water.

By now, the fisherman had the entire boat's attention when he pulled in his line to find a dollar bill on the hook. Dumbfounded, he stared at it.

The comments shouted out were hysterical. "You got a stripper fish by the G-string. Drop it back down!"

"Throw it back, it will be a ten-dollar bill by next summer!"

"For a five, you can get a fin dance!"

"It's much better to catch a stripper than a striper (bass)!"

Tip money blown away

Being a Deck Hand on the *Albatross* is an adventure in itself. You meet all kinds of people and see all kinds of things, and you're always striving to make tips. This included doing some strange things to entertain the patrons if the fishing was slow, such as putting a skate on your head as a hat, or as one of my coworkers did, eat some strange items, including bait and '*Albatross* sushi'.

I remember one trip when a woman went to hand me a $5 bill for filleting her fish, but before I had it in my hand, the wind blew it away from her and over the side. Instead of giving me another $5 bill she simply said "Oh, there goes your tip AYYY!" and walked away. I felt like saying, "Not so fast, you still have to pay me for filleting your catch!"

Annoying phone question

All types of questions are posed when people call to inquire about *Albatross* fishing trips and make reservations. Some calls can be short and to the point while others can be very long and 'somewhat' annoying. Here's one that was particularly frustrating to Chip.

I answered. "Good Afternoon, *Albatross* fishing"

"Ya, hi, um, I am looking, ah, for boat, its name is ....what is that name honey? Oh ya, *Albatross* and it takes people fishing"

"*Albatross* Fishing, how may I help you?"

"Oh, so you are the *Albatross*? What do you fish for?"

"We are a Head Boat in Cape Cod Bay that bottom fishes, but we mostly target winter flounder."

"Well, what are the safety features of the boat?"

For the next forty minutes, we discussed: What do you fish for? (three times) What are your safety features? (four times) Directions to the boat from their hotel? (two times) The procedure for buying tickets and boarding? (two times) Whether the Deck Hands would fillet the catch? What was the best bait to use? Was there parking available? How much did it cost to park? and Whether there was a bathroom on board? (four times).

I was trying to be as polite as possible and at the fifty-minute mark in the conversation, she finally says "Great, do you have room on board for seven tomorrow morning?" Feeling that my patience has been rewarded with a nice payday, I said "Absolutely" and took her information. I felt, in a strange way, that almost one hour of patience was being rewarded with a large booking. But what she said next blew my mind.

"Great! Can't wait to see you tomorrow! My kids and I have been going out on your boat every year for the last twelve years and my kids talk about it all winter! We will see you in the morning!"

Really? Every year for the last twelve and that call took almost sixty minutes? That's an hour of my life I will not get back.

Bloody dogfish massacre

One summer day we had a husband, wife and their two little girls on an afternoon trip. They made it very clear that they were only there for the scenic experience and the sport of fishing. They believed in Catch and Release. They made it very clear they didn't eat fish or any animals, for that matter. At the start of the trip, they requested we throw back all the fish they caught.

That week was very heavy with passengers and dogfish. Their particular trip was full, with 49 passengers standing basically shoulder to shoulder. The dogfish were wrapping up lines all day. We often cut our hands and got stabbed by the spikes in their back fins when we tried to pull the hooks out of the fish. Eventually, we would just bang the dogfish on the side of the boat's rail to knock them off quickly. It would typically snap the hook and we could avoid injury.

Late in the afternoon on this hot, August day, I was very tired, losing my patience and annoyed with this particular family for breaking three poles and asking the most irrelevant questions. They complained they hadn't caught any 'real' fish. I was beside myself because they weren't going to keep them anyway.

So, the little girl hooks another dogfish. Up until that point I was bringing them up onto the deck to take the hook out in a peaceful respectful manner to please them. As I reached down on the deck to grab the hook out of its mouth, the shark was able to bite down and give me a nice mouth print on the side of my thumb. The whole peace-loving, earthy type of façade I was trying to play in front of them, to get a good tip, went right out the window.

I grabbed the shark by the end of the tail and hit it against the side of the boat so hard, over and over in frustration, that its head eventually split in half. It splattered blood all over me until it ripped off the hook and floated away. It was upside down with its insides hanging out, only to be attacked by a swarm of sea gulls.

I apologized to the father and said "We can't save them all". I honestly didn't care at all until I turned around to hand the pole back to the little girl, whose mother was wiping all the splattered blood off her and her sister's face. All three had a look of horror, like I had just committed murder in front of them. Well, I guess in a way I had. Thank God it was the end of the trip but let's just say I didn't get a tip from that family.

Handicapped fishing

We had a gentleman on board that had injured both of his hands in a previous accident. He was right handed and that hand was totally bandaged and unusable. His left hand had some smaller wounds but was partially usable. He was in a fantastic mood, seated at the starboard rail while enjoying a beautiful Cape Cod day.

He hooked up with what seemed to be a very large flounder. Initially, instinct took over and he tried to retrieve it using the fully bandaged right hand. After about thirty seconds he realized that was not going to work so he switched to his left hand. Using a right-handed reel, with a bandaged left hand, progress was slow to say the least. He was managing about one turn of the reel every ten seconds or so, and the fish continued to bend and shake the rod. The well-intended Deck Hand offered to help but he was insistent that he was going to land this fish unassisted. What should have been a ten-second task to retrieve the fish morphed into three minutes or so.

The man seated next to him leaned over and said, "Ya know, when you first hooked that thing I was pretty sure it was under-sized, but I think by the time you get it aboard it will be trophy sized"

The guy with the fish started laughing so hard that all progress stopped for about two minutes. I was delighted when eventually, he landed a very nice winter flounder. The man was ecstatic that he had done it unassisted.

Osprey Captain tricking Captain Dave

In the above chapter on Male Deck Hands, a story was told about the anchor of the *Osprey* snagging a large anchor from an old schooner. As a joke, George, the *Osprey* Captain, called Dave Howes and told him the old anchor had coins encrusted in the rust. Dave became extremely excited over this and met the boat when it returned to the dock. When George finally told him it was a joke, with no coins recovered, Dave was not amused but it gave George and his Deck Hands a good laugh.

Boat congestion at the Albatross loading dock

Chip is a very mild-tempered man and I had never seen him lose his cool with anyone. But one particular morning, as Chip and I went to move the *Albatross* to the commercial dock for the morning trip, we noticed a boat had taken our normal loading spot. This forced us to use the busy town dock adjacent to the boat ramp. As we approached with the *Albatross*, we saw a sailboat tucked up close to the harbormaster's boat and another boat tied up and unattended. The position of the second boat would leave us nowhere to tie up broadside to load passengers.

We had to back in stern-to and tie up perpendicular to the dock to load everyone. Eventually, the guy who owned the nuisance boat arrived. He was not in the best mood but got on his boat. We expected him to move away quickly but he hung around and acted in no rush. Chip finally had enough and yelled down to the guy from the bridge of the *Albatross*. "Well, are ya gunna move, princess? It's all about you today, huh?"

Laughter erupts from the passengers and then the guy on the boat fires back saying, "Who me?"

Chip now yelling back, "Yes you!"

The guy on the small boat goes on to say that yelling at other boaters is real great for business and that he will talk to Chip later. Which Chip replies "We can talk now! Call me! 512-728-2417!" Applause from the passengers erupts again as we pull the *Albatross* away from the dock.

I don't want to give the impression that Chip is a curmudgeon or a jerk. The other guy was in the wrong and justifiably, Chip lost his temper and has not done so since. It was one of the funnier moments I have seen from Captain Chip.

Tossing a bucketful into the wind

George, the Captain aboard the *Osprey*, remembers one day when the only toilet on the boat was out of order, so everyone had to use a bucket. When the boat returned to the dock, it was nearly full and quite 'ripe'. Dave yelled an order to the young, inexperienced Deck Hand, "Go empty that bucket!"

The wind was very strong that day but the Deck Hand did not think about the best (or worst) direction to toss the bucket's contents. He simply walked up to the bow of the boat. Before George or Dave could yell "NO" the Deck Hand tossed the bucket's contents directly into the wind.

George remembers the end result. "It was not pretty!"

Hanging over the side of the boat

You never knew what was going to happen, what you would see nor what you would have to do as Deck Hand on the *Albatross*. Sometimes we hung over the side, with the other Deck Hand holding onto you for dear life, to free the anchor from a lobster pot or trawl. Other times we would dive under the boat to cut fishing line and rope free from the propellers. This was sometimes a result of an '*Albatross* Nantucket Sleigh Ride' when occasionally a pot line got caught in the propeller. At full boat speed, the pot ended up skipping over the waves in back of the prop wash.

Once when the *Albatross* moved away from the dock, we pulled a strong metal cleat out of the dock and it shot by within feet of my fellow Deck Hand, putting a three-quarter-inch dent in the boat when it struck. If someone had been standing in front of that, it would have been all over.

We had fun, but we knew to be aware of safety also. For the most part, we operated like a well-oiled machine, even if the boat wasn't, as I remember a few times working on those engines 'til well into the night.

Fish eyes

Many of the *Albatross* Deck Hands had not yet encountered Asians nor heard of their eating delicacies. One day, a group of Asian passengers proceeded to eat the eye balls out of the freshly caught fish. This freaked out not only the Deck Hands but many passengers aboard. Eels and monkfish were their favorite fish. They even wanted to keep the skates and dogfish.

Enforcing passenger limits

Captain Dave was always careful to abide by the Coast Guard regulations for his Merchant Mariner license as well as the *Albatross*' capacity guidelines and safety requirements. One morning, 48 passengers had boarded the boat so only one more passenger could join on that fishing trip, according to the regulations. As the boat was about to leave the dock, an elderly man and his young grandson arrived and wanted to go on the fishing trip. Dave felt bad nor did he want to turn away the paying customers but explained to the man that he could not take the pair on that trip because it would exceed the per-trip passenger limit for the boat. The man became frustrated and began to verbally pressure Dave. Regardless, Dave had to send the two away because they could not be allowed aboard, together on that trip. He was simply enforcing the Coast Guard's passenger regulation.

The amusing part is that while Dave's intentions were always good, he sometimes came across gruff and insensitive. This was one of those instances. The verbal exchange actually went like this: Near the end of the conversation, the grandfather said, "It won't matter if the young boy comes along."

To that, Dave replied "Yes it will, if he drowns."

'Not what the other passengers wanted to hear, nor the boy. It was Dave just being Dave.

Funny questions from passengers

"Is that the Kennedy Compound?" This is an astounding question because it revealed that this person was woefully ignorant of Cape Cod geography. He was pointing to a very large house situated on the cliff just west of the entrance jetty to Sesuit Harbor, and owned by a gentleman named Bill Stone. Most people know that the Kennedy properties are located in Hyannis on the south shore of the Cape, about ten miles to the southwest of Dennis.

"What do I do if I catch a whale?" The Captain and Deck Hands normally answered "Reel him in." But they really wanted to reply with "Jump over the side."

Is it all water beneath the boat?

While the *Albatross* was anchored for fishing offshore Barnstable, one of the passengers asked the Captain how deep the water was.

"Fifty-two feet" was the response, read from the boat's fathometer.

The man pondered that for a few moments then pensively asked for reassurance. "So, its water, all the way down, for fifty-two feet?"

The Captain was justifiably speechless, thinking to himself, 'What else could be under us?'

Ignorance of fish biology

One afternoon, it became clear that a specific passenger didn't understand fish biology and survival. I was back filleting fish with another Deck Hand during our return to Sesuit. A lady was watching us fillet the fish and throw the skeletons (racks) over our shoulders into the water. Captain Chip made his way back to see how we were doing on time. After about the fifth or sixth rack we had thrown into the water, this lady turns to Chip and asks, "So how long will that take to grow back?" Instead of Chip telling the lady that it will, in fact, not grow back and the fish is dead, he quickly replies with "Oh about two to three weeks, but it all depends on water temperature as that controls how quickly the flesh will grow back".

It was one of the funniest questions I had ever heard, followed by an even better response.

Another incoming phone call

Captain Dave might have had less patience than the 'average bear' when it came to incoming calls about *Albatross* fishing. He much enjoyed the families that came out for leisurely flounder fishing versus the 'hard noses' who would get bent out of shape if they didn't catch a big bag full of fish. Dave recalls one less-than-enjoyable incoming call from a prospective fisherman:

"What's running Cap?"

Dave answered, "Flounder, that's all we catch here in Dennis waters."

"How many can I expect to catch? What's the average per trip?"

Dave anticipated this fisherman would set high goals then be frustrated if the fishing trip fell short by a few fish. He decided to head this potential customer in a different direction. "I think this is the wrong kind of trip for you. We make family trips to catch a few flounders. You should go out on the boats in Provincetown. They'll promise you real deep-sea fishing. You might even catch some wormy codfish."

A few days later, the man called back and proceeded to make many trips on the *Albatross* after that. Dave didn't bother ask if the man went fishing in Provincetown but he suspected so.

Pranks on Fellow Deck Hands

When the Deck Hands became close friends from working side-by-side on the *Albatross* under a wide range of conditions, they would often pull pranks on each other. Add girls to the equation and the pranks got even funnier.

A male Deck Hand enjoyed having Chip's daughter apply sun block to his face and extremities. One morning, the girl played a big joke on the boy by mixing fine, colored glitter into the sun lotion and smeared it all over him, without his awareness of the fancy appearance in the bright sunlight. It was a hysterical show for the other Deck Hands and passengers.

Deck Hands would place live seaworms into the purses of the girls working aboard.

And Deck Hands would drop pieces of clam into each other's cold drinks when they weren't watching. The rule was that if they hadn't seen the placement occur, they were forced to eat it. All the clams were fresh so it wasn't a health hazard.

Night fishing for striped bass in the harbor

Many Deck Hands appreciate the Carrolls for allowing them to 'hang out' on the boat after work. It is typical of the Carrolls' openness and inclusive family spirit. One night, three Deck Hands boated out to the *Albatross* that was at anchor in the inner harbor. They fished for striped bass as the sun set, while drinking 'cool beverages'. One of the Deck Hands didn't have much fishing experience compared to the other two but proceeded to hook and eventually land an average-sized bass. This was no big deal to the experienced fishermen but the other Deck Hand was ecstatic. He was a very 'spirited' kind of guy so he held the fish over his head and kept screaming, happily, and with all types of expletives in celebration of his trophy fish. It's amazing no one called the police because he surely was heard around the whole harbor! A very funny night aboard the *Albatross*.

Dating tourist girls

One Deck Hand's memory: Being quite shy as a youth, I did get up the nerve to ask a few girls for a date that were onboard with their parents. One actually accepted, to my surprise, and I think we went to the Dennis Drive-in Theater. She went back home two days later; never saw her again.

A second Deck Hand's recommendation: I think every Deck Hand was able to get a number from at least one girl that came out on the *Albatross*. The key to flirting was to do it in the morning before you filleted fish and smelled like fish guts.

And once we got older, into our later teens, we occasionally acquired beer from the boat at night and spent time with tourist girls. Also, we'd take the skiff out to the *Albatross* on its mooring and 'night fished' with a girl.

A third Deck Hand's advice: Don't try and flirt with girls after a second trip at the end of the day, you typically don't smell so great.

Fourth Deck Hand: We were too young to date the tourist girls but one of the booth girls gave us a strip show in the cabin on a rainy afternoon. That was a highlight of the summer.

Amusing sights at the harbor boat ramp

One Deck Hand recalls that every weekend, at the end of the day after washing down the *Albatross*, we would watch the nearby boat ramp as many boats lined up to be pulled out of the water by vehicles with trailers. It was worth the free price of admission. Quite often, cars would take ten minutes trying to back their trailer down the long, steep ramp. Once that was accomplished, everyone could see that it was probably their first time trying to get their boat on the trailer.

We witnessed a Boston Whaler still in the water waiting his turn but getting very impatient. His wife was yelling at him because they were going to be late for their dinner reservation. There were probably six other boats ahead of him to get hauled out. His wife kept telling him to bring her ashore so she could get the trailer and try to reduce their wait time. Since there were no places to tie up while waiting, she told him to drop her off at the edge of the natural peat moss banking.

She was a large woman in a very expensive-looking coverup. While he was trying to edge up to the banking, she stood up on the bow holding a line in her hand so she could jump ashore when they got close. He was definitely a novice boat operator. She yelled "Back, reverse" but he hit the throttle rather than putting the engine in reverse. They hit the bank, stopping suddenly and she ended up face first in the mud. Wow, was she mad; especially when she heard us laughing.

After a hard week of work on the *Albatross*, Dave would allow us to join him and his Dad, Skip, in having cold beverages while watching this funny show at the boat ramp.

Similar memories are held by other Deck Hands who watched the frequent antics on the boat ramp, while having lunch on the flybridge of the *Albatross* between fishing trips. Dave and the Deck Hands called it "Boatniks" after the Disney movie of 1970, which was fiction comedy about an accident-prone Coast Guard ensign who had repeated mishaps on the waterways.

18

Safety, Medical and Weather Issues

Safety Issues Aboard the Albatross

The *Albatross* is licensed by the U.S. Coast Guard for fishing trips in Cape Cod Bay. The maximum number of paying passengers is governed by Coast Guard regulations, as well as rules for life jackets, life rafts, flares, horns, fire extinguishers, first aid gear and other safety equipment. The Captain of the vessel is required to give a "Safety Briefing" before or during the first half hour of a trip. And it's the Captain's discretion as to how brief the briefing will be.

Because the *Albatross*: 1) can normally reach the dock within fifteen minutes of an accident, 2) does not operate on the High Seas, 3) does not spend nights at sea, and 4) is almost always in sight of land, the Safety Briefing mustn't be long or detailed. It normally consists of where life jackets are stowed, how to put them on and how to use the head (toilet), so the Deck Hand doesn't have to perform emergency plumbing repairs.

"This is a life jacket. If we're sinking, grab one of these. And don't cut yourself, because I'm the Doc!" Actually, the Captains provide a bit more guidance than this during their Briefings.

To date, the *Albatross* has not sunk, collided with another vessel, been hit by lightning or rogue waves, impounded by the Coast Guard or pirates, caught fire, been swamped by a tsunami, waterspout or hurricane. So far, so good.

With regard to pointed dangers, there have been many instances aboard the *Albatross* when fishhooks have gotten caught in Deck Hands, passengers and even a Captain. Most of the time, the hook can be removed easily but there were times when a barb had to be pushed through a person's flesh and cut off on the other side. Details will not be given here.

Fortunately, there has been no loss of life aboard the *Albatross* in the fifty-two years of operation. A serious goal.

Deck Hand jobs are dangerous!

No one should underestimate the dangers that face Deck Hands aboard the *Albatross*. Hauling the anchor requires care to keep hands and legs out of the line, especially in close proximity to a rotating winch.

As mentioned above, fish hooks can find their way into Deck Hands' hands, especially when passengers yank the line when they shouldn't or when a large fish decides to flop around on deck as the Deck Hand is trying to remove the hook from its mouth – a frequent event.

Another major hazard is when inexperienced fishermen try to cast their hook and weight using a fishing pole. Their first action is to aim the tip of the pole behind them and close to other persons – not good! Next, they use a quick arm action to toss the weight and hook overboard. How better to hook an unsuspecting, nearby person? Well, it happens. But typically, fishhook accidents aboard the *Albatross* are less severe than those aboard Charter Boats where they have very aggressive fishermen frantically casting at fish with long poles and big, half-pound lures having three treble hooks attached. Most doctors and hospitals on Cape Cod have wall plaques with large lures excised from arms, legs and heads of fishermen. At least the hooks used on the *Albatross* are less than one-half-inch across.

Fish too can be dangerous

Passengers on the *Albatross* think fish are slippery and messy; some smell too. Deck Hands know how each species of fish can hurt them. Take for example, the friendliest and most desired fishy caught on the *Albatross* – a small, flat, winter flounder with a tiny mouth and no teeth. A Deck Hand couldn't get his/her finger in its mouth if they tried. Dangerous? Hell yes, if you're not aware. On the right side of the fish at the aft end of the gill case near its anal discharge port, there's a sharp spike (bone) that definitely hurts when encountered. Deck Hands quickly learn the whereabouts of this well-hidden hazard. Nature clearly places a danger where Mr. Flounder doesn't want to be messed with.

Consider the spiny dogfish – a 'shark' to most passengers who lack marine biology training. Shark teeth are expected to be the hazard with these fish but the teeth are quite small, although with sharp points bent outward. The teeth are organized into several rows and are used mostly for grinding rather than tearing flesh.

A more serious threat hides in the two dorsal fins of the dogfish. These fins are situated on the centerline of their back. A large (one-inch long), sharp, mildly poisonous dorsal spine is embedded in front of each dorsal fin. The spiny dogfish uses the spines defensively by rapidly curling its body back and forth to strike its enemy. Deck Hands need be aware of these spines when the dogfish are slapping their tails around. Their mouth is less of a problem whereas the spines hurt when entering a Deck Hand's arm – I know from experience.

Even the lowly cunner (bait stealer) has many hazards – their pointy fins. 'Same for sea robins. And watch out for the dozens of pointed teeth of goosefish (monkfish) and the razor-sharp teeth of bluefish! Each fish species presents its own dangers and the Deck Hands must be careful at all times. They may not talk about it, but they've got to be on-guard whenever a lively fish flops on deck.

Seagulls rarely come aboard the *Albatross* but they can present danger. On occasion, gulls have grabbed the bait from lines near the surface and they immediately become the Deck Hand's problem. Everyone would love to see the hook gently removed from the gull and have it fly away unhurt. But if the bird is seriously entangled in the line and its flight might be impaired, or if it's hooked, then it becomes the Deck Hand's responsibility to solve the problem for the angry beast. This isn't easy, especially when all the bird wants to do is peck at whomever is closest. Everyone should respect the brave Deck Hand who dares grab the bird in an attempt to help it. Realize he'd rather just cut the line but many onlookers might complain, while being unaware of the real danger faced by the Deck Hand!

Medical Issues Aboard

How to remove a flounder hook from someone's hand

Back in the early days aboard the *Albatross*, if a passenger caught a small flounder hook in their hand or finger, onboard first aid would be administered. If the hook could not easily be removed or if the hook's barb was caught in the skin, Plan B would be initiated. After obtaining consent, Captain Dave would take the hooked person into the wheelhouse and stick their hand into the cooler containing beer and ice. After about ten minutes in the ice water, he would push the small hook thru the hand until the barb came through. Then, with wire cutters, he would cut off the barb and back the hook out.

It was a quick procedure for a quick solution, compared to steaming ashore, driving to the doctor's office and having nearly the same procedure administered, albeit professionally and sterilely. Dave would suggest the passenger obtain a tetanus shot the same day.

On a few rare occasions over the fifty-two years of *Albatross* operations, there was no safe medical solution aboard the vessel for a serious fishhook accident, so professional assistance had to be sought ashore for the victim.

Cutting hands while filleting fish

Deck Hands aboard the *Albatross* make extra money each day on the way in filleting flounder. I got pretty good at it, cutting my time down to twenty seconds each fish. You needed a sharp, flexible knife to achieve this speed. The only downside was slicing my fingers by accident. A few times, someone would ask why there was so much blood when fileting. I told them because the fish were so fresh.

I remember that Dave's hands would always be chapped and splitting from putting his hands in salt water all the time. Deck Hands' hands would always be smooth and soft. I figured out at the time that the only thing we did different than Dave was that we always had our hands in quahog juice while cutting bait. There must have been something chemically that kept our hands soft. I suggested to Dave that he should stick his hands in the juice for a cure. He probably was tempted to tell me where to stick my hands too.

Thinking back, Deck Hands are young – that's the reason for soft skin.

Unknown puncture in a Deck Hand's hand

One thing I will never forget, and I have a scar to prove it, was when I got stuck in my hand by God knows what. It was just a tiny pin hole of a wound at first. But within a day, my hand was three times its normal size and the infection was traveling up my arm, fast!

I went to the ER in Hyannis and they brought me right in. The doctor stuck a needle in my hand to numb it but the Novocain spurted out of the pin hole, almost hitting the doctor in the eye. Chip loved seeing that. The doctor next squeezed all this disgusting puss and blood out. Then he cut my hand open and squeezed more out to let it drain. Thanks to modern medicine and antibiotics or I might be gone. Hopefully it'll never happen again!

Bad Weather Encountered on the Albatross

Waterspout

On a very windy day with thunder storms arriving from the west, the *Albatross* and the *Osprey* were fishing off Barnstable Harbor. Winds kept increasing but we were trying to complete the morning trip rather than return to the harbor early due to bad weather. At about 10:30 a.m. Dave called on the radio from the *Albatross*, "Let's go in; it's nasty!" Soon after, he pulled anchor and headed back to the harbor.

About a half-hour later we also pulled anchor on the *Osprey*. As I fired up the engine, a little, old man pointed out from the port side of the boat and hollered "Look!" just as a waterspout passed about 300 feet from the boat. We had never seen one before and have never seen one since.

It temporarily scared the Captain and everyone aboard but the boat was not impacted.

Strong west winds

On many afternoons, my (George's) Father would accompany me on the *Osprey* for fishing trips. He loved to sit in the pilot house and relax as I "worked the crowd". As the boat rounded the west jetty departing Sesuit Harbor, the seas crashed over the bow, soaking the passengers sitting up front.

It was a beautiful, clear day but 35- to 40-knot winds were blowing out of the west. Eventually the boat reached the target fishing area offshore Barnstable and dropped anchor. The seas were six to eight feet high and it was very uncomfortable for everyone.

As we fished, one-by-one the passengers dropped like flies, sea sick. Out of 37 passengers and two Deck Hands, all were sick. One of the Deck Hands was in a fetal position in the life raft on the flybridge.

After two hours or so, I announced that we probably should head in. There were no objections and one-by-one, the whole bunch came back to life. The boat was full of 'chum'.

Shawney watches the Albatross (temporarily) disappear amidst the waves

When Shawney was running the business, starting in 2006, Kevin Huck was Captain on the *Albatross*. On days when the weather forecast was marginal or bad, and a decision needed to be made whether the seas would be too high for a fishing trip, Shawney always left the decision to the Captain. She knew he had the most experience.

One particular day, the winds were 35 knots from the north. Shawney still recalls. "It was the scariest trip ever." When the *Albatross* left the dock, she drove her car to where she could see the boat leaving the harbor and beginning to pass between the two outer jetties. "The waves were so high, at one point I couldn't see the boat as it went into the swell between two waves."

The big boat did return four hours later but Shawney worried during the whole trip.

Passenger 'discomfort' during a rough-weather trip

Kevin also remembers the rough-weather trips. "There were some days we never should have been out there. We had green water breaking over the bow of the *Albatross*." (The mariner's way of saying they had a wave of solid water coming over the front of the boat versus just some sea spray.)

"When we were assessing the sea conditions at the dock before heading out, I told all the passengers it was going to be very rough. One man said 'This is the only day we can go, so please let's go.' Other groups agreed, so we left the dock.

When we were offshore, it was very rough and most everyone was uncomfortable. A woman started yelling 'You should never have taken us out.'

I calmly reminded her and the entire group that I had told them the weather was going to be bad and they all agreed that we should go. No one was forced to stay aboard.

Not wanting to hear that, the woman next said 'We're going to die!'

No, you won't die. You'll just be uncomfortable for four hours."

A wave over the Deck Hand's head

I was pulling up the anchor at the bow of the *Albatross* when a large wave came straight over the bow and over my head too. I was under water for a split second. I couldn't believe a wave was big enough to come over the bow, in Cape Cod Bay. On another day, my fellow Deck Hand was off helping with the Sesuit Harbor Regatta on a seventeen-foot Whaler and they caught massive air, with the whole boat out of the water. 'Goes to show the surprising waves that can occur in the Bay, even in summer.

Another Deck Hand's memory of bad weather with Captain Huck

There were a few days of bad weather that I remember on the *Albatross*, with Captain Huck. He was a Mate on an Alaskan Crab boat prior to moving to Massachusetts. He had a very different opinion of what was too choppy, rough and storm like.

One rough day I remember saying to myself, 'Whose idea was this?' As we headed through the harbor and past the Sesuit Harbor

Café, there were big rollers breaking in front of the Yacht Club. I knew it was going to be a bad day. We made it out to the fishing grounds but the fishing was slow and almost every customer had puked in the head, or worse. At one point I went down below deck with a bucket and puked a few times myself.

I'm pretty sure it was Shawney who decided we wouldn't be doing an afternoon trip. One of the happier moments in my life.

And yet another Deck Hand's memory of rough seas

I remember a few times when we went out and it was rough, really rough. Once, I was standing at the bow and blue water came through the holes in the gunnel like fire hoses. And water came over the bow too. That was enough to make the hair on the back of my neck stand up!

When we caught three footers on the side of the boat, everything that wasn't tied down, including passengers, would fall to one side and then to the other as the boat rolled. That's when I would give my speech, 'If you are going to be sick, do it over the side.' as I was hosing out the head (bathroom).

Expressions for vomiting aboard a boat

If you're going to lose your lunch, warn your close neighbors with a sense of humor. Tell them you'll soon be:

"Chumming"

"Tossing your cookies"

"Feeding the fish"

"Calling seals" (the sound is the same: urh, urh, urh)

"Letting up the cargo"

"Calling Ralph on the porcelain phone"

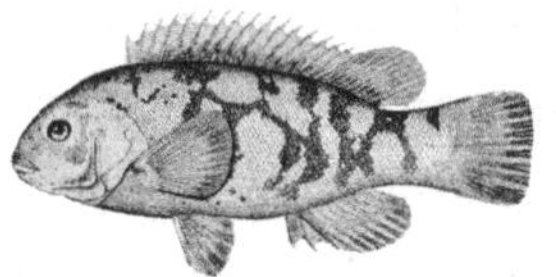

19

Lessons Learned and Careers of Deck Hands

Lessons Learned

For the Deck Hands who worked on the *Albatross* and *Osprey* over the past fifty-two years, the experience was enjoyable, significant and rewarding. Many have shared the following lessons that have and continue to help them throughout their lives:

- As a first job for many young Deck Hands, leaning how to follow orders and work responsibly.
- Learning the duties of a Deck Hand, including safe line handling and anchoring.
- Teaching passengers how to fish and handle their hooks and fishing gear safely, especially around other persons. The young Deck Hands often taught adults.
- Learning how to interact courteously with the general public.
- Acknowledging that respectful interactions with strangers can be rewarded by tips.
- Developing a good, focused work ethic that proves useful in pursuing other jobs.
- Providing care to injured and seasick passengers, which has led to medical, paramedic and firefighter careers for many Deck Hands.
- Amassing maritime skills and experience as a basis for careers in the marine industry.

Below is an assortment of candid comments on Lessons Learned from *Albatross* Deck Hands:

"My time on the *Albatross* over the past six years has provided some of the best memories and times of my young adult life. Chip and the other fine people I have worked with, and for, will always remain in my life, not just as friends but as family."

"Dave knows more about operating on the water than anyone in the region. A real merchant seaman. He taught me everything about boat operations and trained me for my Captain's license."

"The job with Dave gave me a whole new, unselfish look at dealing with the general public which helps me to this day."

"I learned how to interact and deal with many different types of people that paid money to go fishing on the *Albatross* during their summer vacation. This helped during my responsibilities working for the Town of Yarmouth and dealing with paying customers at the Town's beaches each summer."

"The *Albatross* helped me develop life-long communication skills. To think I was 11, 12 and 13 years old as a Deck Hand, teaching 49 people on each trip how to fish and be safe. This was pretty cool. Learning to communicate with passengers and try to make tips has definitely helped me become the person I am today, in a good way."

"Dave helped me get my Captain's license, teaching me at his house and with hands-on boat training. He gave me a great start."

"The experiences I had as a young kid on the *Albatross* and later working for Dave as a Deck Hand helped shape who I am as a scientist and educator."

"Fish guts, clam juice and grease aren't gross – they build character."

"If I had the experience I did within the harbor and on the *Albatross* earlier in my adolescence, I think I would have seriously considered pursuing a marine-related career."

"My Mom made my Dad take me out fishing on the *Albatross* when I was six. He hated it but I loved it. Later I became a Deck Hand, working for Dave. He taught me all about seamanship and boat handling."

"Don't tell an Irish Captain that he doesn't make sense. He'll just yell at you in a mix of accents: Irish and some ancient Celtic language."

"Working for Dave on the *Albatross* was a learning experience. It also prepared me for the next tough boss I'd meet in my career. Dave taught us everything on a boat and about being a hard ass."

"One summer, Dave, Skip and myself traveled daily to Mattapoisett to help the boatyard while building *Albatross III.* I learned a lot about working with fiberglass for boat construction."

"A truly formative, fun and gratifying experience which stoked my already-burgeoning love for ocean life and seafaring."

"A beer at the end of a long hot day never hurt anyone, and five more should always be customary."

"Some of the best and effortless striper fishing is below the *Albatross* at the dock."

"Tourists are unique; that's the only way to put it."

"I had a lot of good lessons out there."

Careers Following an Albatross Deck Hand Job

The *Albatross* Deck Hand job has been an effective springboard for many Cape men and women who later pursued marine careers across diverse segments of maritime commerce, security and support services, medicine and ocean research. Their successes are a tribute to the training and mentorship they received during their early years aboard the *Albatross*. Examples of Deck Hands' careers are given below, absent the surnames of individuals:

Merchant Seamen

Nate is presently Third Mate aboard offshore drilling vessels working for Rowan Companies.

Steve attended Maine Maritime Academy and is now Chief Engineer aboard offshore service and supply vessels for Edison Chouest Offshore.

Mike attended Massachusetts Maritime Academy and worked as Chief Mate on oil tankers in Alaska.

Dan attended Massachusetts Maritime Academy and works as Chief Engineer on tugs operated by Kirby Offshore Marine.

Pete is an Able-Bodied Seaman (AB) aboard tugs for Kirby Offshore Marine.

Andrew is enrolled at Massachusetts Maritime Academy and is an active Deck Hand on the *Albatross*

U.S Navy, Army and Coast Guard

Greg attended Massachusetts Maritime Academy then joined the Navy. After 20 years of active duty, he retired as a Commander. Later, he raised his Merchant Mariner's license to Master and is now a civilian Captain on a 950-foot vessel of the Navy's Military Sealift Command in the western Pacific.

Stefan is a Specialist at the Massachusetts Army National Guard.

Chris is a retired Warrant Officer from the Coast Guard and is now a Captain for TowBoatUS in Bass River.

Marine Research and Education

Owen is Director of Marine Fisheries Research at the Center for Coastal Studies in Provincetown.

Josh studied at the University of New Hampshire and now works as an Environmental Scientist at Partner Engineering & Science Inc. in California.

Dave is nearing completion of his Ph.D. in Aquatic Evolutionary Ecology at the University of California, Santa Cruz, focusing on human-induced thermal effects on fisheries.

Scott worked at the Woods Hole Oceanographic Institution (WHOI) in his twenties and participated in deep-ocean research cruises up to seven months in duration. Later, he earned his M.S. and Ph.D. degrees in Ocean Physics, conducted research around the globe and is now retired from a corporate position managing 125 environmental scientists. He recently obtained his 100-ton Captain's license.

Tony studied Marine Biology with emphasis on genetics and worked on underwater habitat studies in Key Largo for NOAA. He is now working for a defense contractor specializing in network security programs.

Ben is currently working at WHOI as a Senior Mooring Technician, designing and deploying oceanographic moorings around the world.

Connor is studying Environmental Sciences at the University of Maine.

Coastal Marine Businesses and Commercial Fishing

Marc is a Captain at Barton and Gray Mariners Club which operates a fleet of Hinckley yachts along the East Coast.

Danny attended Massachusetts Maritime Academy and is now manager of the Northside Marina at Sesuit Harbor.

Mike is owner/manager of Dennis Parasail & Jet Ski of Cape Cod.

Jeff has his own sportfishing business on Cape Cod and in Rhode Island.

Tim attended Massachusetts Maritime Academy and works at Northside Marina.

Medical

Tammie began her career in education, receiving a B.A. in Elementary Education and Technology followed by an M.S. in Environmental Studies. Then she was a Paramedic and Fireman for a few years. Recently, she became a Physician's Assistant after earning her M.S. in that field also.

Cait obtained a B.A in Molecular Biology and her M.D. from Rutgers University. Today she is a practicing M.D. of internal medicine at Tulane University's Medical School.

Leathan is a First Lieutenant in the Army National Guard and presently works at Coastal Medical Transportation Services.

Amanda obtained her B.S. in Nursing and is now a Registered Nurse at the Cape Cod Hospital.

Matt is owner of Cape Cod CPR and First Aid Training as well as a Firefighter/Paramedic at Yarmouth Fire Department.

Linnea obtained her M.S. in Nursing Education and is presently working on her Doctorate of Nursing Practice. She also works in the Cardiac Unit at Cape Cod Community College and teaches nursing classes.

B.B. was a medic in the U.S. Army and presently works as a Deck Hand on the *Albatross*.

Firefighting and Paramedics

Kevin Huck is a Captain at the Yarmouth Fire Department.

Glen is a retired Captain of the Hyannis Fire Department.

Nick works as a fireman/paramedic at the Yarmouth Fire Department.

Albatross Deck Hands and Captains Reunions

In January 2017, a small reunion of *Albatross* Deck Hands and Captains was convened at the Dennis Highlands Golf Course restaurant. Roughly twenty past Deck Hands and four Captains participated at this impromptu gathering. Deck Hands represented 1965 through the present, some not having seen each other for fifty years. It was a very enjoyable event! Photos from this reunion are presented in this chapter.

Another reunion will be convened in late July 2018. Notices will be posted on my *Albatross* Facebook page (https://www.facebook.com/AlbatrossBoys) and in local newspapers. Hopefully we will attract a majority of the one-hundred Deck Hands and many Captains. As I acquire additional information on the careers of Deck Hands, I will publish a revision to this book with demographic information.

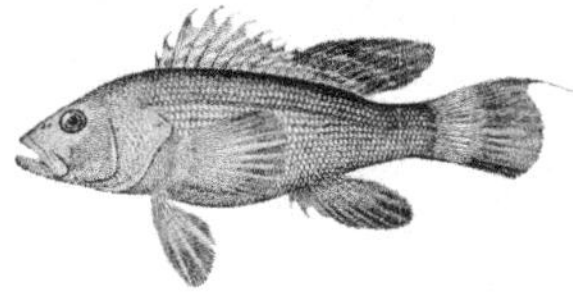

20

Additional Seagoing Activities

Marine Life Cruises with Mass Audubon

For many years, the *Albatross* has conducted Marine Life Cruises in Cape Cod Bay in collaboration with Mass Audubon, the largest Nature Conservation nonprofit organization in Massachusetts. The cruises are typically conducted on Wednesday evenings from 6 to 8 p.m. during summer months. For more information about the Marine Life Cruises on the *Albatross*, contact: http://massaudubon.org/wellfleetbay

On each cruise, Mass Audubon provides a trained Naturalist to explain the marine biological communities that reside in the water column and on the seafloor in Cape Cod Bay. Samples of numerous species are collected during the cruise using a variety of sampling equipment including: plankton net, otter trawl, scallop dredge, sediment grab sampler and lobster pots. Species include fish, plankton, crabs and shellfish. Samples are dumped on deck for participants to inspect and touch the many 'flappy things' and 'creepy crawlers' as described by the crew of the *Albatross*. Responsible marine conservation is practiced by all.

Decades ago, Dave Howes conducted *Albatross* trips to show local students various aspects of hands-on Oceanography. These morphed into the Marine Life Cruises of recent years.

Sunset Jazz Cruises

In the summer of 2017, Chip Carroll initiated Sunset Jazz Cruises aboard the *Albatross* on Thursday nights beginning at 6 pm. These cruises offer patrons a pleasant ride in the Bay while watching the sun set in the direction of the Cape Cod Canal. Contemporary jazz and pop music is played by a two-piece band, Seabreeze, consisting of a trumpeter and a guitar player, with flute and large conga drums substituted on certain songs. George Machon, the 'brass section', is famous in *Albatross* history, having worked for Dave Howes back in the mid-1980s as Captain of the *Osprey*.

I suspect Seabreeze will master the song 'Albatross', originally created by Fleetwood Mac in 1968, and play it on future Jazz Cruises.

Ash Scattering Ceremonies

Cape Cod Bay has touched the lives of tens of millions of people and many wish to have their cremation ashes spread over the Bay. Captain Chip Carroll offers an informal environment for family and friends to spread the ashes of their loved ones from the stern of the *Albatross*. At-sea celebration of life is a positive experience and one that will be remembered by all participants.

In summer of 2017, I made arrangements with Chip for a ceremony aboard the *Albatross* to spread the ashes of my best guy friend from Brewster. His widow coordinated directly with Chip who was very compassionate during the planning. Thirty family members and friends boarded the *Albatross* at 5:30 p.m. for a slow cruise to the southeastern portion of the Bay where my friend and I had spent many days fishing and clamming since the early 1970s. One relative had built a small, wooden replica of my friend's fishing boat specifically for use in the ceremony. A small box containing his cremation ashes were placed in the replica boat, set afire and released to the sea as the *Albatross* moved away slowly. We circled the burning replica for a half hour to celebrate my friend's life, then headed back to Sesuit Harbor after the sun had set. The small flaming, ceremonial boat could be seen up to a distance of one half-mile. Overall, it was a respectful and enjoyable ceremony that everyone appreciated.

Chip has mentioned that other ash spreading ceremonies have been performed equally well and compassionately, with family and friends paying their respects to the loved one in the calm environment of Cape Cod Bay. Each ceremony is unique, as directed by the immediate family of the deceased, and Chip is very cooperative in accommodating individual requests.

21

Wounded Warriors Fishing Trips

In August 2017, Captain Chip Carroll and his wife Shawney were awarded a plaque for their continuous support in efforts to touch the lives of Cape Cod veterans. Although both Chip and Shawney are retired from the Air Force Reserves, they continue their dedication and generosity to service men and women of the region. A small ceremony in appreciation of their efforts was conducted aboard the *Albatross* during one of the Sunset Jazz Cruises.

Below are descriptions of fishing events the Carrolls conducted aboard the *Albatross* specifically for Wounded Warriors.

Wounded Warrior Event – September 2013

Captain Chip Carroll hosted veterans aboard the *Albatross* for a fishing trip in Cape Cod Bay. Below are excerpts from an article on the Westover Air Force Reserve Command website:

"On September 16, Lieutenant Colonel Charles 'Chip' Carroll hosted twenty-seven wounded veterans aboard his fishing boat in Cape Cod. Throughout the day, schools of fish and loud laughter filled the boat…. 'This job is unique in that I can give people happiness,' he said. Since buying the boat in 2006, Lt. Col. Carroll and his family have been able to do just that. In recent years, he's begun to provide this service to those who have served.

He recalled the day in the summer of 2009 when he was contacted by the Director of Spaulding Adaptive Sports. 'When I got the phone call, she explained that I had the only boat large enough to accommodate the needs of wounded and disabled veterans,' he said. 'She asked if I would be interested in hosting a group aboard the boat. I was ecstatic. I said to her, 'Do you know what I do for a living? (meaning a pilot for the Air Force Reserve) I would be absolutely thrilled to have them!'

In the spring of 2013, Lt. Col. Carroll received the Thomas Francis Meagher Award, which is given annually from the local chapter of the Cape Cod Veterans Association that recognizes work done for veterans in the Cape Cod area. 'I was nominated by the harbormaster where we keep the boat because he knew of our work with the Wounded Warriors.'

The warm, sunny weather and over 200 fish reeled in – including an electric ray – made a perfect day aboard the *Albatross* in Cape Cod Bay.

'The fishing event was one of the best events I've been to in a long time. This is the first event in which I've been able to meet other vets like myself and make some new friends while having a good time,' said disabled Army veteran, Kal Kent. 'It was life-changing.'"

Wounded Warrior Event – September 2010

Adapted from an article at www.prweb.com, September 25, 2010:

After a year of planning, a group of volunteers and non-profit organizations sponsored the first ever Wounded Warrior Weekend on Cape Cod. Participants passed an honor guard of retired veterans as they walked to the fishing boat *Albatross* at Sesuit Harbor. A bagpiper on the dock played anthems from each branch of the armed forces, and a crowd of onlookers gathered to watch. Fourteen veterans from ten states made the trip to the Cape to experience bonding, camaraderie and fun. They camped, fished, kayaked and golfed – and they also healed, if just for a little bit.

The Wounded Warrior Project and Disabled Sports USA teamed up with CAPEable Adventures Inc. and the Rehabilitation Hospital of the Cape and Islands (RHCI) to organize the weekend. The RHCI offer activities that can help the incredibly brave men and women achieve a sense of normalcy.

A participant said, 'Everybody's got a different story. But we're really all the same. I'm making new friends and we're all bonding. This is a great event.'

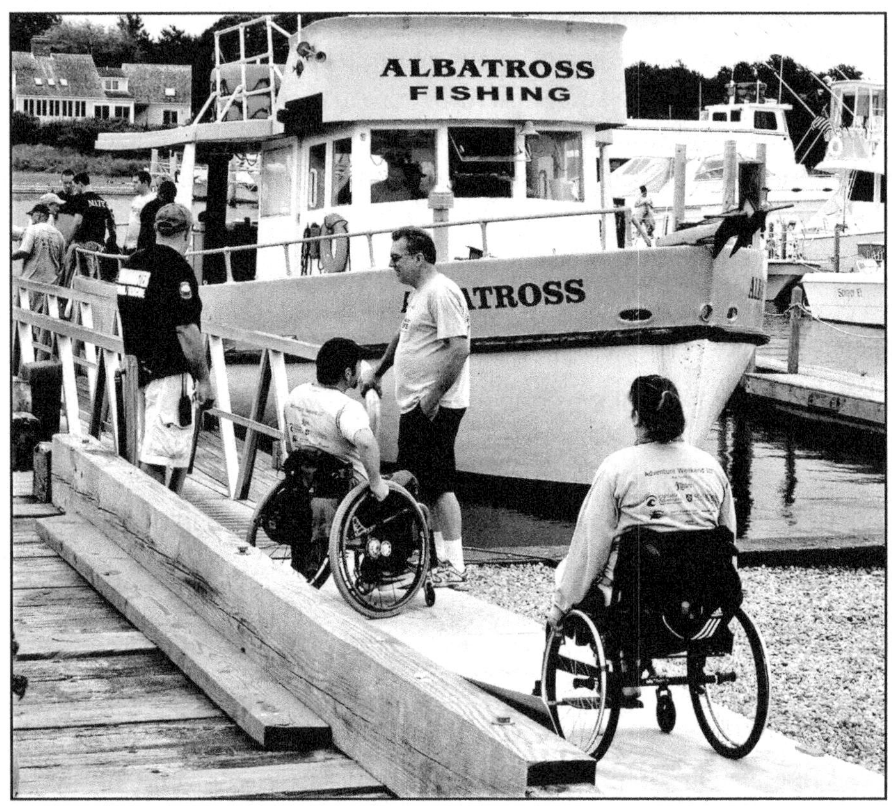

Chip Carroll and his wife, Shawney, own the *Albatross*. He's active Air Force Reserve; she's retired Air Force Reserve. Between them, they've logged 55 years of service. So, when RHCI came calling, the Carrolls never hesitated. 'Absolutely, count us in,' Chip recalls. 'Whatever you need.'

Chip's 'day job' is flying huge Air Force transports packed with military gear into war-zone hotspots like Kandahar and Kabul in Afghanistan. But on this day, Chip helps bait hooks, unhook fish, and chat up his guests of honor.

When the fishing trip was over, one of the volunteers spoke to Chip, 'Well, I just want you to know how special this has all been. I just don't know how to thank you.'

<u>Links to volunteer organizations</u>:

Wounded Warrior Project – www.woundedwarriorproject.org

Spaulding Rehabilitation Hospital of the Cape and Islands – www.spauldingrehab.org

CAPEable Adventures, Inc. – www.capeableadventures.org

The Carrolls have conducted eight such trips for the veterans, nearly one each year, in coordination with the Wounded Warriors, Spaulding Adaptive Sports and the Cape Cod Veterans Association Post 333.

List of Deck Hands

The following list includes names of *Albatross* Deck Hands as provided by Captains Dave Howes and Chip Carroll. Names are in approximate chronological order starting at the top of the left column, going downward, then the middle column from top to bottom, etc. Some names may accidentally be misspelled. My goal is for all past Deck Hands to contact me so I can obtain their years worked and first-hand experiences aboard the *Albatross*, plus information on their careers. When the full demographics of Deck Hands have been compiled, I will publish an update to this book and convene a reunion for all Deck Hands and Captains.

Scott McDowell
Scott Munson
Chris Myland
Dean Emery
Greg Goolishian
Toby LaVigne
Chris Cooney
Dan Schadt
Patrick McDowell
Rich Carter
Glenn Coffin
Daniel McDowell
Tom Forest
Tammie Howes
Terry Lawler
Dave Smithers
Tony Wilkins
Liam Cahill
Scott Gesner
Christian Philbrook
William Chase
Nate Provost
Chris Boyle
Sean Marcarelle
Mike Dutch
Jake Berry
Todd Turcott

Brian Collins
Dan Burke
Craig Phillips
Mike Tarantino
Steve Milligan
Kevin Loski
Chris Schilling
Owen Nichols
Brian Trudnac
Peter Milligan
Mark Hutchings
Mike Close
Jake Crowell
Chris Spero
Joe Griffith
Dan Gilrein
John Lowery
Matt Emery
Jeff Viamari
Pete Gilrein
Cait Martin
Caleb Crowell
Dave Hodsdon
Ben Pietro
Eric Anderson
Nate Severdija
Peyton Preston

Nick Ciocca
Matt Regan
Ryan Smith
Nick Napolitan
Leathan Doig
Linnea Carroll
Sarah Carroll
Mark LaCroix
B.B. Reardon
Reggie Donnithorae
Connor Huck
Bradford Emery
Dave Fryxell
Spence Mohr
Lacey Titus
Stefan Napolitan
Andrew Gemme
Ben Gardner
Josh Cain
Joe Cahill
Amanda Gemme
Eddie Brunton
Nate Olsen
Chris Gaetani
Tim Willet
Mark Smithers
Nilo Gerwatowski
Jared Blake

Acknowledgements

Special recognition goes to Dave Howes for his daring launch of the *Albatross* fishing business in Dennis, Massachusetts. Tourists in the Dennis area had limited funds back in the mid-1960s but Dave initiated the business with a modest boat, a very 'salty' Father and young Deck Hands who loved fishing in the Bay. Input from Dave and his two daughters, regarding the history of the boats and the business, was essential for this book.

Chip and Shawney Carroll and their two daughters kindly shared stories about acquiring the *Albatross* in 2006 and thereafter, running it as a successful family business. Their positive energy has added much to the lives and careers of Deck Hands under their direction during the past decade.

It has been very enjoyable interacting with dozens of Deck Hands who worked on the *Albatross* over the past fifty-two years. Hearing stories and experiences from both eras of *Albatross* ownership has been enlightening.

Kevin Huck from the Yarmouth Fire Department shared his stories of working as Captain under both Dave and Chip.

Greg Goolishian, who is a true Master of Oceans, described Dave's significant role in his pursuit of a maritime career.

George Machon still enjoys his multi-faceted involvement with the *Albatross*, having started thirty-three years ago.

Thanks to Patricia Walker for her encouragement in the early stages of the book concept.

Kevin of King Technical Services, North Falmouth, MA, designed the excellent cover for the book, provided layout services for the interior, and is my website Master.

And warm appreciation to Susan Bacoyanis, my darling, for her encouragement, writing guidance and editing of the manuscript.

Lastly, and most significantly, I thank the North Dennis Firemen who administered CPR to me on Scargo Lake while I was in total cardiac arrest until the Dennis Ambulance arrived with defibrillation equipment. That was in February 2007, as my daughter remembers well, because she too participated with CPR as I lay on the frozen lake. We all should be thankful for First Responders.

Acknowledgements for drawings and photos

Kevin King for graphic services for figures and photo enhancement,
Fish images from the NOAA Photo Library.
Photographs were provided by the following individuals, listed in order of those who provided the most photographs:

Chip Carroll and family

Scott McDowell

Dave Howes and family

Patricia Walker

Dave Fryxell

Dan Gilrein

Author Biography
Scott E. McDowell

www.scottemcdowell.com

scott_e_mcdowell@yahoo.com

Dr. McDowell grew up in the village of Dennis on Cape Cod. He worked as the first Deck Hand on the fishing boat *Albatross* starting in 1965. Following three years working for Captain Dave Howes, he worked summers as skipper and tuna guide on a private sportfishing boat catching giant bluefin tuna from 400 to 700 pounds. Their boat won the Cape Cod Tuna Tournament when he was seventeen and landed sixteen giant tuna before Labor Day in 1970.

Now he is retired from a successful career in physical oceanography. He enjoys living in Miami and cruising the Florida Keys and The Bahamas aboard his sixty-foot motor yacht ***Someday Is Now***. Today, his top priority is writing non-fiction on maritime topics, as well as fiction novels of undersea espionage and oceanography.

Education

Ph.D. Physical Oceanography, 1982, University of Rhode Island

M.S. Oceanography, 1973, University of Michigan

B.S. Chemical Engineering, 1972, University of Massachusetts – Lowell

Author

Marinas – Complete Guidebook for Marina Selection
Non-Fiction, 2015, Atlantic Publishing Group, Inc., 288 pages,
Florida Authors and Publishers Assoc.- 2015 Gold Metal Award
Category: Sports

Deep Vorticity – Huge Swirling eddy deep in the Atlantic Ocean
Fiction-Suspense, 2015, Amazon Publishing, 315 pages

Captain, 100-Ton Master – Licensed by the U.S. Coast Guard

Oceanographic Research

As a physical oceanographer with extensive experience in the analysis of currents, tides, waves and water quality characteristics, Dr. McDowell conducted numerous measurement programs in coastal and deep-ocean environments. Examples from his thirty-year career are given below:

- Conducted deep current measurements and seafloor geological studies in the 20,000-foot deep Vema Channel in the western South Atlantic Ocean. [Johnson, D. A., S. E. McDowell, et al., 1976. J. Geophys. Res., 81(33), 5771–5786]
- Participated in research of active seafloor volcanoes for two months at 63° South latitude in the Antarctic Ocean. Encountered thirty-foot seas and eighty-knot sustained winds.
- Made the first-ever discovery of a sixty-mile-wide ocean eddy (Meddy) one mile below the surface in the western North Atlantic Ocean, which spawned research on mid-ocean eddies over the next two decades. [McDowell, S.E. and Rossby, H.T. 1978. Science, Vol. 202. No. 4372. pp. 1085-1087]

- Collaborated in a five-year, multi-national oceanographic measurement program of currents and dynamics of the entire western North Atlantic Ocean. Was Principal Investigator for determining the geographic origin of dozens of mid-ocean eddies that were discovered during field measurements. [McDowell, S.E. 1986. J. Physical Oceanography, Vol. 16. Issue 3. pp. 632-652]
- Managed a two-year field measurement program to assess currents, tides, water depths and meteorology in the vast Yukon River in northwest Alaska. The one-hundred-mile-wide delta was very remote and previously uncharted.
- Conducted current measurements in the Gulf of Thailand beneath gas production platforms owned by a U.S. petroleum company, for the purpose of understanding strong, unpredictable forces on their vertical drilling equipment.

His project experience includes oceanographic studies on both the East and West Coasts of the United States, the Gulf of Mexico, the Caribbean, the Bering Sea of Alaska, the Mediterranean, the Gulf of Thailand, the South Atlantic and the Antarctic Ocean.

Oceanographic Industry Experience

Dr. McDowell was initially employed by the Woods Hole Oceanographic Institution (WHOI) to participate as scientific crew on a seven-month geophysical investigation in the South Atlantic to assess the Mid-Atlantic Ridge and the volcanic seafloor of the Antarctic Ocean. Soon after, he conducted oceanographic measurements aboard a Naval vessel during a seafloor study in the Caribbean while Dr. Robert Ballard (Titanic discoverer) conducted simultaneous measurements within a research submarine operated by the U.S. Navy. During his three-year period at WHOI, Dr. McDowell participated in numerous deep-ocean studies and was co-author on research papers published in oceanographic journals. Proudly, he participated in over three-hundred days of mid-ocean research during one fifteen-month period.

Employed by private industry for the next twenty-seven years, Dr. McDowell conducted complex oceanographic measurement programs for state and federal agencies as well as commercial clients, worldwide. During his final years of employment, he managed a Marine Sciences and Environmental Planning Division with one-hundred-twenty staff located in seven offices nationwide. Forty staff had M.S. and Ph.D. degrees, exemplifying the high caliber of the organization he led, with annual revenues of $23M from professional services conducted. His responsibilities included technical and financial management, strategic planning, business development and recruiting but oceanographic work was always his key interest.

Young Scott with 650-pound bluefin

Sponsor

Sesuit Harbor Café

Classic Cape Cod Clam Shack
Family Owned and Operated Since 2000

Specializing in lobster and local seafood
Outdoor dining overlooking Sesuit Harbor

Breakfast Lunch Dinner

Open during Summer

Located at 357 Sesuit Neck Road, East Dennis

Call: 508-385-6134

sesuit-harbor-cafe.com

Sponsor

Sponsor

1661 Route 6A, East Dennis, MA

Custom creations, unique gifts, something for every room in your home!

Open everyday March to December!

Sponsor

Sponsor

Dennis Parasail & Jet Ski

Most fun and safest parasail rides on the Cape
Enjoy beautiful views over Cape Cod Bay

We also offer Jet Skiing with new
Yamaha 3-person skis

Activities based at Sesuit Harbor in East Dennis

For reservations call: 508-385-8359

Email: dennisparasailing@gmail.com

Facebook: DennisParasailJetSki

ALBATROSS

ALBATROSS Fishing - Field Notes

Date Family members Captain

ALBATROSS Fishing - Field Notes

Date	Family members	Captain

Made in United States
North Haven, CT
24 January 2022

15167277R00104